# MARKETING MOXIE FOR LIBRARIANS

# MARKETING MOXIE FOR LIBRARIANS

## Fresh Ideas, Proven Techniques, and Innovative Approaches

PAULA WATSON-LAKAMP

LIBRARIES UNLIMITED™

An Imprint of ABC-CLIO, LLC

Santa Barbara, California • Denver, Colorado

**Library of Congress Cataloging-in-Publication Data**

Watson-Lakamp, Paula.
  Marketing moxie for librarians : fresh ideas, proven techniques, and innovative approaches / Paula Watson-Lakamp.
     pages cm
  Includes bibliographical references and index.
     ISBN 978–1–61069–893–1 (pbk : alk. paper) — ISBN 978–1–61069–894–8 (ebook)
  1. Libraries—Marketing. I. Title.
  Z716.3.W38  2015
  021.7—dc23              2015001875

ISBN: 978–1–61069–893–1
EISBN: 978–1–61069–894–8

19  18  17  16  15      1  2  3  4  5

This book is also available on the World Wide Web as an eBook.
Visit www.abc-clio.com for details.

Libraries Unlimited
An Imprint of ABC-CLIO, LLC

ABC-CLIO, LLC
130 Cremona Drive, P.O. Box 1911
Santa Barbara, California 93116-1911

This book is printed on acid-free paper (∞)

Manufactured in the United States of America

# CONTENTS

# ACKNOWLEDGMENTS

I've been at this marketing game a very long time. The reason why is because it is FUN! I love seeing happy, smiling faces coming away from a special event, to have a small child ask you about a book they saw on a display, or to have someone see your nametag at the grocery store and say, "Wow, I can't believe all the things the library is doing! Keep it up!" These make all the sleepless nights and crisis emails worth it. I have been very fortunate to have some wonderful mentors encouraging and teaching me along the way as well as plenty of anti-mentors who told me something couldn't be done, which of course made me want to do it even more! Many thanks to my social media mentor, Nick Armstrong at WTF Marketing (yes, you read that correctly) for keeping me growing as a marketer. Extra thanks to my husband, who has spent many hours toting chairs and setting up tables—the poor man didn't know what he was signing up for by marrying me—and my kids, who always smiled and waved while I left them at the fair booth while I ran to print more flyers. Thank you for your support, I love you all, and you have made my life the best special event ever.

# INTRODUCTION

"Build it and they will come" is an old adage that works for the world of libraries. The building of a library in a town has always been seen by townspeople that they have arrived—that culture, civility, and democracy had come to their town and they were living, breathing members of that democracy. No matter if they had paved streets, running water, or outhouses—they had a library.

In most cases a library is an interesting semigovernmental entity—not quite a nonprofit, many times treated as the ugly poor cousin of a city government. Hey, you have to fill the potholes first, right? No two libraries seem to be organized or funded quite the same. The only thing that they all share is their fundamental mission to bring information to the masses—they were doing it way before Internet search engines! In order to be relevant in the next 100 years, libraries need to ramp up their marketing moxie! Begin to think like a business, not be complacent in being the poor cousin.

Libraries are a special breed of business—yes, I used the "b" word. We can no longer sit back and wait for people to walk through the doors in awe of the wonderful services we can offer them. Whether you call them patrons, members, users, or customers, you need to know who they are, how you can retain the ones you have, and how to get more of them.

Beginning with the basics, you will be able to use the information covered to start building your library marketing skills and see your way to ramping up your moxie to set your library apart from its competition.

Whether you are a standalone library on the Great Plains, a multibranch system on the East Coast, a one-person marketing office, a multiperson office, or a library director that has marketing added to their lengthy job description, it's time to set up a plan for your library, and along the way, have some fun and don't take it all too seriously. This book will show you how.

## HOW TO USE THIS BOOK

In doing the research to build my own moxie marketing skills, I have read hundreds of books, white papers, and websites and attended webinars and presentations on all things related to marketing. There are many extremely wonderful resources on each of the topics that I have brought together in this book. Many business-type books are meant to be read from start to finish, but I have organized this book in such a way that the busy marketing person can look at the contents for a specific area of concern and dive right in to find a starting point, a reminder, or a tip or tactic that they can put to use right away and not have to finish the book first. I wrote this book to help the library marketing person who just received an email from their director that the board of trustees wants to see a 10 percent increase in circulation by the end of the year, and it is that person's job to make that happen!

So get started, dive in, don't panic, and remember that being a moxie library marketer is all about experimentation and fun!

# GETTING YOUR LIBRARY IN ORDER

## BRANDING—YOUR LIBRARY'S IMAGE

"Branding is for cattle," touts the poster that hangs in my office. The term *branding* was adopted many years ago by public relations and marketing professionals to try to put a handle on a group of thoughts around external communications.

Just like there are differences between marketing and public relations, branding is not just about your logo. Sure, having an awesome logo helps, but to understand the term *branding* in its fullest context, go with this definition by marketing expert David Newman (2013): "A brand is a promise of an experience. Period." So you need to make sure you and your staff know what you are promising before you can try to communicate it to others. Your brand is the way you communicate to your customers, members, patrons, staff, whatever you want to call them. It is the way your members or customers know that in every branch they go into in your system, they can expect the very same thing, like going into a national fast-food chain that is in every state in the United States.

One person cannot be a *brand manager;* this is up to every single person in the organization. I have run across libraries in the same systems that, because of the way they are managed, have very different brands. Is the first thing you see when you walk through the door a sign about the *rules*, or are you welcomed by a volunteer greeter asking if they can help you? Many have very active children's areas with things to climb on and tactile experiences to sing about. Others have lines of puzzles and quiet cubbies for book reading. If you have a three-year-old that has been cooped up at home for days during a snowstorm, which *promise* would you head for? The problem arises when the mom and child come in expecting to blow off a little steam, playing inside the giant book mobile or spinning the letter whirligig, and a staff member gives them *the look*. You know the look—somewhere between the shushing look of the past with the condescending look of *you must be a bad parent*. It is the act of not fulfilling the perceived promise that makes people feel uncomfortable and makes them not trust you. On the other side, if you have a smiling staff person say to you, "Wow, you are full of energy today. I know of a great game you can play in the library and then check it out to take home and play." Fulfilled positive promises make good library supporters. This perception flows into all aspects of what the library is about, which brings us to the dreaded mission statement.

## MISSION/VISION

How many hours have organizations taken, how many thousands of dollars on consultants have been spent, on coming up with a *perfect* mission statement? This statement, along with the future forward *vision* statement, is supposed to inspire your employees, to address your core values, and tell who you are, what you do and for whom, what you want to be, and what your brand promise is. Wow! That is a lot of power given to a few words. Not to say that preparing mission and vision statements is not important; they are a very good way to change organizational culture, to ensure that management and the board of trustees are heading in the same direction, and to help the staff feel empowered in forging the future. Many times, though, after hours and hours of discussion and many hundreds of dollars, the statements are printed on posters, hung in offices, put on the website, and added to the annual report, never to be discussed again. In order to simplify the process and to make the statements memorable, a good idea is to treat it like the plot of a good human interest story. Ask these three questions:

- Why do you exist?
- Who do you serve?
- How will they be impacted by your work?

This customer/patron-centered way of defining your library not only enables you to look outward and not inward, but helps you learn to tell your story by telling the stories of your customers. Tell the story about the young entrepreneur who used your grants and foundations database to get a million dollars in startup money for a new project. Talk about the grandmother who used your free Internet and Skype to connect with her grandchildren who live on the other side of the world. Show how a young man taught himself Spanish by reading the Spanish-language books in the children's area. That's the best way to market, ever!

Tell these stories through creative words and thoughts, and these will help you to target your audience and your message. Use these messages throughout your marketing channels, and they help to formulate your brand.

## LOGO

Your customer-centered messages lead to your logo. If your library is part of a city or county government, you may not be able to use anything besides what has been established for that entity. But if you are fortunate enough to be able to create your own identity through visual representation, this is one of the most fun processes you will go through. This representation is the cornerstone of all your brand promises; it should take into account all of the brainstorming statement work that was done during the mission/vision meetings. For this reason, hire a professional designer! Do not have a contest, have the lead librarian's nephew who draws come up with it, or do anything else to cut corners, or money. In the end, you will get what you paid for, and it won't be good. Also, try to find a local marketing firm and/or designer who is knowledgeable about your community and your library; they can cut out a lot of stereotypical library visuals because of their involvement within the community. Look for other visual identities in town and obtain recommendations; doing your homework will help to make the process go much smoother. When sending out the request for logo proposals, be specific about what your needs are, and interview the candidates just like you would when hiring a staff member. The firm you hire needs to *get* what a modern day library is; if the answer to the first question is "I love to read," run!

In working with a designer, do not have a group of more than five people working on the committee. When our library went through this process, we had the communications director, the president of the board, a staff member, the president of our Friends group, and a community member. This committee worked with the designer to come up with a recommendation that was rolled out to the rest of the staff and the community at the same time. I know some of you are thinking this would never work in your library, but if the committee does its job right, it will evaluate the designs on objective criteria, such as:

- It is memorable and easy to recognize
- It works in both large and small formats
- It works and is legible in both color and black and white
- It is unique
- It stands the test of time
- It stands up to use across multiple mediums such as website, social media avatar, print, etc.
- It doesn't attempt to literally represent the mission and vision (think about how any libraries have a book in their logo and now are trying to change their library's perception to digital formats)

I guarantee your logo will not be liked by everyone—some people don't like the color orange, and some don't like purple. But if the committee can come to a consensus of "like," not "love," the logo will work the way it is meant to be—a visual representation of your "brand promise." By hiring a professional to do your logo, you will also get important information that should come along with it; these are usually called Graphic Style Guides. These guides can help you to set boundaries around how the logo is used; a color dictionary with RGB, CMYK, and HEX definitions for use in printing, and online channels and any extras that are part of your brand identity, such as certain tag lines and how they can be used, or other graphic elements to be used in your marketing. These should all be identified in your Request for Proposals (RFP) process.

Some resources for seeing the logo design process at work are found at http://richpowell .com/journey-of-a-logo, where artist Rich Powell shows his concepts for the Randolph County Public Library; and http://www.brandsoftheworld.com/awards, which shows entries for their logos of the year contest. Graphic design online publications *HOW* (http://www.HowDesign.com), *AWWWARDS* (http://www.awwwards.com), and *LogoLounge* (http://www.logolounge.com) not only showcase great design, but also have articles about trends in logos and designs.

**MOXIE TIP** When deciding on a logo design, you should have the designer also add in the design for the social media avatar in a square and/or round format. This symbol in many ways will become more valuable to you than the complete logo and will be used on all your social media platforms.

Another word to the wise: Some library systems with multiple branch locations let their numerous locations formulate their own logos. Don't let that happen! The process and accomplishment behind doing a branded strategy and identity will bring your library to the forefront of the businesses in your community. Letting one branch take over their identity will diminish that accomplishment. Just look around at any high-profile business, whether a fast-food restaurant or a retail chain; their logo and identity relate to the brand promise that you will feel when you walk through the door, and you want that positive impression for your library as well. As the marketing director, you need to be the brand sheriff and have a deputy assigned to each branch to keep the law and order of the logo. Staff who have been doing their own fliers for years will not like being told that they must now use a new template in town, or that they can't make the logo a different color to fit with the library color scheme. It might take time to get everyone in line to see the bigger vision, so stay strong, and make sure the library director is behind you, understands the marketing principles, and will back you up for the good of the organization.

## COMMUNICATIONS AUDIT

Doing a communications audit as part of your marketing program provides an essential guide to help you understand how all of your communications and marketing plans work together. Taking the time to sit down and really think through all the communications work will also help you to understand where your time is being spent and force you to look at some time-management questions of whether you may need to hire someone else to do it, or whether to let it go.

A communications audit is different from your marketing plan audit. In a marketing audit, you make sure that you are reaching the right groups of people through the correct mix of communication channels. If you can't describe your target audience, or if you know your audience but are not getting results you want, then you need to do a marketing plan audit. In a communications audit, you focus on what *communication tools* you are using and how well they are working for your marketing strategy.

To begin your communications audit, pull together all of your communications from your marketing channels from the last three months, whether in print, broadcast media, or online. This may seem like a lot of work, but gathering this information not only will amaze you at the amount of work you do, but, as an added benefit, can help you when you go in for that pay raise!

Print out your blog posts, newsletters, Facebook updates, posters, press releases, print ads, and everything else you've done over the last three months, so that you can have everything together to look at one time. Don't forget to include your website as one of your major communication channels. Website best practices have an additional set of questions farther down.

Pick out a peer library or other business that you think is really doing communication right. Gather communications from this organization so you have something to compare your pieces to. Write notes about their work, and why you think they are rocking it! Your judgment will be subjective, but thinking about how you rate against your peers in best practices helps you to look at the larger picture of your work. In reviewing your pieces of work, some good questions to ask as you move forward are:

- Do all of the communications appear to be from the same organization?
- Are the subject lines of your emails captivating?
- Do they look professional?
- Ask, so what? Ask yourself, is the content relevant to the people receiving it?
- Do you use consistent logo and masthead on your newsletters and eNewsletters?
- Do all your social media channels use the same name as your website?
- Do your communications show what your mission is?
- Do your communications feel genuine, that real people are behind them?
- Do your social media home pages have a consistent look?
- Do you use library lingo terms such as eResources, Database, Circulation?
- How often do you ask people to take action (sign up, donate, join, check out)?
- What is the overall tone of the writing style? Serious or fun?

Additional audit questions for your website:

- Does your logo appear at the top of every page?
- Do you have features that change to make the home page more exciting?
- Is your blog seen as part of your website?
- Is your site built responsively so it changes depending on the device it is being viewed on?
- Is the contact information easy to find?
- Is your site visually interesting?
- Do you include pictures of people and stories?
- Is there an easy way to sign up for eNewsletters?
- Do you have all your social media icons visible?
- Do you have a donation button that stands out?
- Do you have Google Analytics attached to every page for metrics tracking?

Look at the communications from your "idol" and ask these same questions. You might want to give a one-to-five rating on each of the pieces, theirs and yours, to give yourself a way to see how you are doing. Do a spreadsheet with your ratings for each question on it to give yourself a visual to look at.

## Analytics and Metrics

Next, look at the analytics and/or metrics for all of your communications to see how they are doing. You should already be tracking these monthly, so pulling this information should be easy. If you are not tracking the metrics for your communication channels, this is a great exercise to force you into making that happen!

Create an Excel spreadsheet (see Table 1.1) listing your communication channels down the first column and putting the months of the year across the top row. Then go through and start filling in the information that is most valuable to you for each channel. On the last column of the top row, add a space for notes or goals. Start filling in each of the last three months of information for each of your channels. For Facebook, you might put in *Likes* or *Engagement* numbers; for your print newsletter, you might put in number printed/number of cardholders; for email, you could put in signups and opens or unsubscribes. Think about what your goal is for that channel and what information is necessary to know whether it is working or not. In the last column, give the channel a one-to-five rating again. For a listing of metric term definitions, see the Glossary.

### What's Next?

Now look at your spreadsheets, answers, and ratings. What are the areas that you are really doing right? These can help to inspire other areas. What areas are on the other end of the spectrum, and which ones are rated three, or the middle? Look at the highest-rated channels, and ask yourself why they are working. Are these the ones you are most comfortable with, so you spend more time on them? Do you have a better strategy for these channels so that they are easier to do? Do any patterns emerge that you can use to boost the lower-rated channels? Can you see any as a total waste of your time because none of your customers are engaged with them—maybe something you have been doing for a long time, or something that your director has mandated? I know many library directors who jumped on the blog bandwagon and now do an update every six months when they get around to it, wasting the time of your busy, information-overloaded audience checking for new posts.

For now, set your short-term goals on your findings, and pick one a month for the next six months. Don't worry about the middle-of-the-road channels until you decide what to do about the ones on the bottom. Maybe you need to drop doing Twitter, or maybe you need to do a better job of getting people to sign up for the eNewsletter. Learn what tactics and content you need to pull together to make your goals happen, and add these to your marketing plan. Chances are that taking care of the channels on the bottom of your rankings by using best practices from your top-ranked ones will naturally drive up those middle ones, especially if you have some you can stop doing or can delegate to someone else.

### STRATEGY OR MARKETING PLAN

When I get together with other marketing and communications professionals, the word "strategy" always comes up. I know many professionals who make their living writing up plans, strategies, and tactics for businesses. But ultimately, marketing or communication strategies basically boil down simply to this: if you don't let people know what benefits a library can add to their lives, they will stop utilizing libraries. Sure, this sounds simple, but we aren't just selling a widget that will make everyone's lives better, are we? Because we have the advantage or disadvantage of being many things to many people, pulling together a cohesive plan can be overwhelming. Libraries must continue to prove their worth now more than ever as the competition from other businesses becomes more prevalent.

Table 1.1

| Social Media Metrics | January | February | March | April | May | June | July | August |
|---|---|---|---|---|---|---|---|---|
| Website (Total Visitors/Unique Visitors) | | Total: 190,079 | Total: 190,079 | Total: 186,042 | Total: 171,651 | 169,337/ 82,148 | 182,710/ 86,902 | 138,914/ 72,910 |
| Blog Visitors (Total/Unique) | 0 | Total: 0 | Total: 97 | 197/138 | 148/107 | 158/126 | 191/126 | 259/215 |
| Facebook Likes | 1,506 | 1,677 | 1,784 | 1,802 | 1,857 | 1,881 | 1,930 | 1,977 |
| Twitter Followers | 1,096 | 1,135 | 1,186 | 1,186 | 1,279 | 1,309 | 1,375 | 1,442 |
| Pinterest Followers | 215 | 224 | 251 | 262 | 285 | 291 | 299 | 305 |
| YouTube (Subscribers/Total Views) | 7/918 | 7/871 | 7/897 | 7/917 | 8/938 | 8/942 | 9/958 | 9/963 |
| Email: Children's (new confirmed contacts/unsubscribe) | 9/40 | 12/29 | 7/8 | 5/11 | 9/27 | 48/18 | 46/18 | 18/36 |
| Email: Teens' (new confirmed contacts/unsubscribe) | 5/4 | 6/6 | 6/4 | 4/6 | 6/8 | 17/5 | 10/12 | 7 111 |
| Email: News & Events (new confirmed contacts/unsubscribe) | 24/16 | 16/16 | 15/9 | 18/18 | 14/20 | 29/14 | 22/19 | 21/18 |

## Where Do I Start?

Plans can be as complicated or as simple as your needs are. If you have a staff of five, you may need to delineate in the plan which person will do which tactic. If it is only you, you can just write down what the highlights are to keep your focus. Many organizations begin with a SWOT analysis (Strengths, Weaknesses, Opportunities, and Threats), which helps you identify what your specific strategies and objectives should be. I recommend doing the SWOT analysis with a group of community members, separately from the staff. Many times the staff thinks they know what the public wants, but the public can surprise you. If staff sees the 60 people coming to storytime every Thursday morning as a strength, and your community group says they see it as a weakness because you are missing the working parents, you can use this as an opportunity to find out more and build a marketing strategy around it. Make sure your community members are library users and nonusers and are from varied backgrounds, ages, and socioeconomic status.

After your SWOT sessions, the management team (including you) should boil down all the information to three or four main goals. These goals can be similar to your libraries' strategic plan goals, but with the difference that they should be outward and customer-focused. For instance, a library-focused goal might be, "The library will create an environment where innovation is encouraged." In order to make the goal customer-focused, you could say, "Identify services that contribute to an innovative library experience"; then you can go about defining what an innovative library customer experience is based on evaluation of current programs and services. If your sessions identified that your community needs added workforce help such as resume writing and online job applications, then you can brainstorm the best way to get the word out about what services your library offers to fulfill these needs. Including the library management will help them understand the marketing plan from their own perspective and will help give you direction in order to make sure that staff buys in on the plan.

## Marketing Plan and Content Calendar

Both of these terms get thrown around in the marketing world, but what are they? Do you need them? How do you do them? I often get asked if I have them, do I use them, do you need both, and what the heck they are, anyway.

### *Marketing Plans*

A simple definition for marketing plan is a written document that describes your marketing efforts for the year. This doesn't have to be as detailed an undertaking as it looks. The main reason for doing a plan is to help you keep on track with your library's goals. It is a plan—a *to-do* list of sorts, and a way to help you define goals and results that set you up for success. Try writing a plan using each of these steps for no more than six projects; even better would be three yearlong projects. The plan usually includes:

- A short description, one page, of your current campaign, **program**, or **service**, and a **SWOT** (Strengths, Weakness, Opportunities, Threats) analysis of the service. If you don't detail the whole process, at least describe the threats or challenges to help you define where your difficulties in meeting your goal might occur. Depending on who is going to use the document, you might also include any history you might need, how the project started, whether you have ever done a similar project, etc.

- In one page or less, list what your **goals** are for the year. This is where your overall strategic plan comes into play. An example might be: A goal is to increase the amount of children coming to storytime at each session by 25 percent by the end of the year, or to create an online form off of the home page of the website to gather customer satisfaction feedback, or to increase the "likes" on your Facebook page by 50 percent by the end of the year.

- A bulleted description of **who** you are marketing to. Who needs to take action? This is easy for academic or special libraries, but for public libraries, it can be challenging. Try to break down who exactly you are looking to reach. The term *target audience* has been redefined in some marketing circles to include *audience segmentation* (see below), which asks you to define your audience in greater detail. This can be very helpful to library marketers when we run into the "This event is for everyone!" scenario. An example of an audience segment might be stay-at-home parents and caregivers of children under four years old.

- Next, list what marketing **strategies** you plan to take to reach each goal, along with the corresponding **tactics** you will use to make them happen. Along with describing the strategy, it might be helpful to add a **benefit statement** or primary message to use in your marketing. Using the preceding example of increasing storytime attendance, you might say your strategy is to include a special book giveaway at each storytime, and that your tactic will be to use your email list of parents to promote it. Benefits to parents could include quality family time, early literacy, parenting skills, etc.

- Finally, you need to add your **budget** or costs associated with each of your tactics. Keep in mind that this also includes staff time and anything else needed to make your goal a reality.

Marketers often also add in:

- **Objectives** and **evaluation** of how the strategy and tactics did or didn't work.
- **Responsibilities**—who is in charge of doing what and when? If you are a one-person department, this is you! But also consider how you might get staff involved with WOMM (Word of Mouth Marketing); or whether you can hire your neighbor's teen for an afternoon to drive around town and hand out flyers at child-care centers. Even if you are the only responsible party, this will help you plan your year. Many times after developing a new strategic plan, the management asks that everything be done in the first quarter. If you have a plan with your goals spaced out on your timeline, it will be easier to regroup when unexpected things come up.

These plans can be as long as 20 pages, or as brief as a one-page spreadsheet. Find a format that works for you and that you won't just put in a binder and forget. Use a format that you can easily explain to those who want to sidetrack you.

Start out slowly, until you get a feel for how you are going to use the plan. Remember that your strategy and time allotment are closely linked. If your strategies involve learning a new email system to be able to send email to those new parents, then you need to make sure you add the time it will take to learn the system into your timeline. See samples of marketing plans in the Appendix.

Now you can get into the nitty gritty, the fun stuff of doing the work. This is where your content marketing and calendar comes into play.

## Content Marketing

Content marketing refers to the technique of creating and distributing relevant content to attract and engage a clearly defined target audience with the objective of driving an action (Content Marketing Institute, http://contentmarketinginstitute.com). The term *content marketing* is all the rage, but the concept has been around for years. The main key to content marketing is that you are looking to understand your audience and give them valuable information that they want, when they want it, and how they want it. As you put together your marketing plan with your overall goals, think about the goals that your content is trying to drive—for example, driving your customers to sign up for your eNewsletter so that you can learn what internal links they click on, and then in turn, send them more content that relates to their interests. You are using your content to build a relationship with your audience. You want your customers to engage with you and feel like they are part of the library, gaining them as loyal fans and advocates.

### Content Calendars

Doing a content calendar will help you to further define your audience, decide what channels you will use and how often you will post, and highlight any special themes for the month or season. Putting together a calendar will also let you find any gaps where you need to fill in with *evergreen content*, or content that relates to all audiences or seasons and can be used any-time. You also want to highlight the content that can be repurposed. For example, you can take your blog post and clip a quote from it to use on your Facebook page; then take the post, add in some visuals, and turn it into a presentation on a document-sharing site; then have someone read the post for a podcast, etc. Another way to remix your content would be to edit it to relate to a different audience; change the lead-in with a different first paragraph or quote, or change the perspective of who is telling the story. Many times after I write a blog post, I sit down and write three Facebook posts and five tweets designed to send people to look at the blog post. I add all of those pieces to my electronic content calendar to ensure that the message is consistent, then copy the content from the calendar onto the channels for ease of posting, tweeting, etc. Learning to write with this sort of repurposing in mind will make your job easier and help you to be able to add relevant information through more channels.

Creating visual content calendars is great fun for those of us who are visual. You can use poster boards with bright-colored markers, online spreadsheet calendars with color coding to be shared through Google Docs, or a calendar that is used as part of your email system some of the various ways to keep yourself on track. Experiment with what might work for you and your team. I use a large Post-it note board in my office for an overall glance at a six-month time frame, then I narrow that down to a shared monthly spreadsheet calendar in Google Docs. I highly recommend using an electronic version of your calendar so that you can copy and paste the content into your media channels without having to retype them. You will learn how much data needs to be defined on your calendar to make your marketing plans run smoothly. You can put headings on your spreadsheet layout such as the topic, who is in charge of writing it, the channel it goes on, the link that goes with it, what audience it is being sent to, etc.

After you map out your marketing plan, take each of your tactics and address how you will do each one. Start with three of the basics—who are you talking to, or your target audience; what is your message; and the delivery method or communication channel (for a sample, see Table 1.2).

**Table 1.2**

| Audience | Message | Channel | Date | Action | Image | Status |
|----------|---------|---------|------|--------|-------|--------|
| Who are you targeting? | Think 140 characters or less | Facebook, Twitter, Blog, Newsletter | When does it go out? | What do you want people to do? Share? Join? Come? | Image URL to go with message | Is this in the works or done? |

What goes out via email, and what channels are being used to promote the author event? How are you driving your customers to read your next blog or sign up for the new eNewsletter? When does this all happen, and who's going to make sure it happens? Taking the time to do a content calendar will control this process and will be worth it!

**MOXIE TIP** When designing your content calendar, don't forget to leave room for the things you can't predict as well as some space to add in some experimentation, such as doing some polling, surveys, headline A versus headline B testing with your email system, etc.

*Target Audience versus Segmentation*

The *general public* as a target audience no longer works, because there is no one general public. This broad term needs to be broken down even further, or segmented. A handy way to think of these segments is to come up with personas for three imaginary friends. If you are out walking your dog, these might be the three people you meet walking down the street. Think of them while you are writing your content, and it will make it much easier not only to write, but to market to those people. When writing, try to emphasize what is important to them; identify their interests, how they like to get their news and information, and how often, as well as what information would be applicable to their lives. Doing this also helps your content be customer-focused.

If you have never done a sample persona, here are some questions to answer about your imaginary friend:

- Name
- Gender
- Age
- Job/Title
- Daily Activities
- Responsibilities
- Concerns
- Needs
- Aspirations

**Basic Rules of Segmentation:**

**MOXIE TIP**

1. Demographics and lifestyle—where they live, marital status, income, age, children.
2. How they behave—whether they are library users or nonusers, check out print materials only, mainly check out eBooks, or come to programs but never check anything out.
3. What their needs are—busy two-parent working families need convenience, teens need somewhere to escape to, immigrants need a place to learn English.

In general, you probably have a good idea of who your segments are in your community by demographic criteria. Try to get beyond the demographic data into the behaviors associated with their library use. Some sample segments might include: customers who want only digital content, customers who want only print content, customers who come to programs but never check out books, or customers who come in only to use the computers or wireless system. Getting deeper into your customer behaviors and using these segments will help your marketing efforts because you will be refining who you are talking to and what their needs are.

After you know who your target audience or segment is, decide what your message is. This is where you put a key message in 140 characters or fewer relating to the benefit that segment will receive. Next, decide what action you want people to take when you want them to take it.

### Media or Communication Channels and Content

Your media or communication channels are your delivery methods. Think email, posters, website, social media, etc. In planning the content to post through these channels, make sure you repurpose it in at least three different ways. Pull out a quote from your blog post and add it to your Facebook post. Then take the photo from your blog post and add it to your Instagram feed. Use your headlines in your online newsletter as Twitter posts. Curate your content from other sources.

Many marketers like to use the 70/20/10 rule for social media. Seventy percent of content should be about other information, not about your library. This could include local happenings, author information, silly videos, blog posts, etc. Twenty percent should be about interacting with your audience. These can be things like polls, questions, and comments. And 10 percent consists of library promotion, events, services, etc. Try as I might, I can't quite make this work because I have over 60 programs a month to get the word out on; but it is a noble baseline to start from. My content mix seems to vary by season as well as by what the social media analytics show me. I always watch my monthly analytics and add more of a certain type of content if I see people are really engaging with it (sharing, liking, commenting, etc.).

**MOXIE TIP**   Create a shared online marketing language cache file where you can store your key messages, mission statement, style guides, content calendar, personas, and any other things that you and your staff might need so that you are all in the loop and your library is readily available. (This is described further in Chapter 9.)

## SURVEYS

"To find out what our members want, let's just do a survey." In my world, this suggestion rolls around about every six months. With online survey tools like SurveyMonkey that are user friendly and affordable, the world has become survey crazy! I have been part of some very well-put-together and well-thought-out surveys, as well as some that grew and decidedly had a life of their own, and gathered tons of data that were never used.

To use surveys effectively, you need to add them into your marketing plan and your content calendar on a regular basis. There are consultants who specialize in surveys and who can help you hone the perfect survey for what information you need to gather. If you don't have the budget to hire a consultant, do some research into doing surveys before you start sending them out. Find the logical thinker on your staff and ask them to help you work on the questions. Writing good survey questions is an art form. If you are writing the questions yourself, research the best way to ask a question so that you are not inadvertently swaying the response answers. A good information source is SurveyMonkey (http://www.surveymonkey.com), which includes a guide to writing survey questions off their website. You also need to make sure that the questions make sense for the information you are gathering, and you need to keep in mind what you will be doing with that information. You could ask a three-question survey at the end of a program to gain insight into (1) where they heard about the program, (2) whether they would like to see more of this type of program, or (3) whether they learned something new that they can now use in their lives. These three questions can help you determine the value that this program has in people's lives and whether it should continue or be expanded.

As mentioned in the previous paragraph, asking the appropriate survey questions for what you want to find out is an art; it is also a science. In the sample questions above, Question #1 is a great question that will help to ascertain how your marketing efforts are working, especially if you are sending out information through 10 different media channels, or if you are trying to decide whether to discontinue doing one of those channels, such as your print calendar. Question #2 doesn't help you at all, because people will always say yes to a program they have attended; a better question would be, "What other types of programming do you attend at the library?" This will help you with your segmentation process of learning about your customer's behavior. Question #3 is always good to ask, not only because it helps you tell your story of why the library is important, but also because it makes the customers think about what makes the library important to them. You won't get many answers to Question #3, but the ones you do get may be priceless.

Some things to consider when writing your questions are:

- What is the goal of the survey? If your goal is too general, you will not get any response that will help you.

- Write your question down in two different ways, and think about what type of response you would get from each question, and which question will give you information that is actionable. For example, you could ask: "Do you use the library frequently?" or "In the past seven days, how many days did you use a library service?" As you can see, the second question will give you better, more specific data to use.

- Watch out for library jargon that people might not understand. Take the word *collections;* some people think of that as the people who come after you if you don't make your loan payment; or programming might be seen as a reference to computers. For example, you could ask: "Do you own a tablet or PC?" or "Do you own a tablet or personal computer (e.g., laptop, iPad, Android tablet)?"

- Avoid leading questions or those taken out of context, such as "Would you like the library to continue to offer XYZ?" If people have never used XYZ, how do they know whether it should be continued?

- Keep survey lengths short, 6 to 10 questions, and have multiple-choice answers for them to circle or check. This will make it faster for them and easier for you to tabulate.

- Watch out for open-ended questions or ones that have too much opinion involved such as "Do you think the library offers enough storytimes? Yes or No." Everyone has a different opinion on what enough is, and knowing that 75 percent of those surveyed said there were not enough doesn't help you understand anything that you can take action on.

- Test your survey before distributing it widely. Give you survey to a few people to see if the results are what you wanted. If they are not, rework the questions and hand it out again. Doing a little upfront work will save you from realizing too late that you forgot to ask something important.

How often should you do a survey? This is a tough question. Because of the ease of doing surveys, especially online surveys, look at your content calendar and see where they make the most sense. Many times, libraries do extensive, assessment-type surveys once a year, so they can use it to judge how their strategies connected to their strategic plan are doing. Surveys run for other purposes should be short, no more than five questions, and sent out or performed every other month. Paper surveys should be manually added into a database or Excel spreadsheet file, so they can be used to measure results of future endeavors. Again, make sure that the information you collect directly affects one of your goals or strategies; otherwise, why are you doing it?

## FOCUS GROUPS

Focus groups are another vital part of your strategies to get to know your customers, and these should be performed a few times each year. This type of informal but structured gathering can bring out meaningful and valuable information. If you are the person facilitating the group, be sure to have someone else there to take the notes, as it is impossible to do both. A focus group works best when the members have a common denominator that bonds them. For example, invite people who are new to the area, or moms with children under two. When the group is brought together from a unified segment of your customer base, you will be able to do more with the results. There are many ways to facilitate a focus group. Here is a simple way that I have found to help facilitate people sharing.

First, decide if the group is made up of people who are already friends of your library—in other words, people who check out books, know you are there, and think you are an important organization. Or are they fans who love you, are in every week, devour all your programming, and are dying to help you? Or, lastly, are they outsiders, people who recognize the building and perhaps have brought their child in for a special book for school, or to use the restroom?

Depending on which of these three types of supporters your focus group falls into, you can design your questions to get the most out of the feedback session. You can find out this information by preinterviewing these people via phone or an online survey. This will also help you weed out any people who may consider themselves the experts on your organization and run rampant with the opportunity to tell you all of the things you need to fix. Doing a little upfront work helps keep the focus groups, well, focused.

After you have selected people who have a commonality and have brought in an assortment of people from your three supporter groups:

- Give everyone a pad of sticky notes and have them write down **three goals** (one on each sticky note) that they have for the community. Have them add these to a poster board on the wall titled *Community*.

- Next, have them write down **three challenges** faced by the community that are keeping it from attaining the goals. Have them add these to a poster titled *Challenges*.

- Then ask them what **conditions** need to change in order for the challenges to be overcome and the goals attained.

- You can then walk from poster to poster and ask people about the ideas without putting a certain person on the spot. Have your note taker write down any emerging themes or patterns and the words that people use to describe their community.

Summarize the exercise by telling a story and using their responses to find common ground. "We began by saying that we wanted a community where [fill in the blank with the goal]. But we face [fill in the blank with the challenges]. So if we want to reach our goal, we need to create [fill in the blank with the change to be made]. Does that sound correct? Then let's discuss what your library can do to facilitate this change."

Working from a commonality and giving the group a specific focus rather than just asking "What do you want the library to do?" will help you get honest feedback. Whether it is something for the teens to do to keep them out of trouble, or a public transportation system that is lacking for people to get around without cars, you will receive valuable insights from people on what their needs are and how the library can work to find solutions to these needs, such as afterschool programs for teens or a books-by-mail program for people who can't get to the library.

## OTHER WAYS TO GAIN INSIGHT

Another way to gain insight into your customers is to look at your website analytics and what they tell you, along with your other social media channels. These metrics can show you how many people view your website, click-through rates to other pages, more-frequently-looked-at pages, and more. Gather this information and store it in a format that you can easily access to help you see not only different behaviors, but what questions to ask if you want those behaviors to change. Watch your social media pages for mentions. You can set up automatic monitoring on keywords and have them saved automatically. This also helps in knowing how your customers refer to services that you provide through words they use to describe it. Don't forget to ask other library marketers about what they are doing and trends they see, especially those with similar demographics to your system. If you are a small library close to a metropolitan system, ask if, for a small fee, your library data can be added into any data gathering they might be paying a consultant to do. We are all in this together, and communities of library marketers through ALA listservs, state organizations, and others are always willing to share. Even better, get involved with a local nonprofit that serves your same population, like United Way or the YMCA. Go in together to conduct surveys and focus groups that will help both organizations and save you money.

**MOXIE TIP**  Data gathering can be overwhelming! The biggest step is just starting. Pick four areas such as your Facebook engagement (the number or percentage of people who like, share, or comment on your content), and track them for four months to see what you can learn. Then decide whether this metric is helpful in driving your marketing strategies, or whether you should do something different.

## MEETING YOUR CUSTOMERS

In many ways, marketing is more of an art than a science. Being able to track, label, compare, and quote is the best way to be accountable to your stakeholders, but sometimes you just have to go with your gut. Recently, as I was sitting alone eating lunch in a popular restaurant and working on my content calendar for the next month, jotting down some thoughts about what I could write about for our blog, I overheard the group of four at the table next to me actively discussing an upcoming city council proposal about limiting the use of plastic bags in grocery stores. I glanced up to see my perfect focus group for an idea I had on writing about a new gardening and composting book I had just read. I jotted down notes on the group: two were in their 20s, two in their late 30s/early 40s; three men, one women; one was making points about hurting the local economy, another was talking about the pain of remembering his bags when he went into the store, and still another was talking about recycling of plastic bags and how long it takes for plastic to decompose. Then, I heard my opening! One asked, "I wish I knew how those bags made from cornstarch are working." I slipped out a copy of my business card that has the "Ask-a-Librarian" contact information on it, went up to the table and introduced myself, handed them the card, and said that we could help them find answers to their environmental questions. "Cool! Thanks!" he said. I went back to my seat and wrote on the content calendar to post on the plastic bag controversy. The point is, sometimes you need to get out of your office to know what is happening in your town, what people are really talking about, and what the library can do to help them.

By now you may be thinking, there are only 24 hours in a day to get my library in order, and this all sounds great, but how on earth am I going to do it all? There are some wonderful resources out there for you. I know you can find them because of where you work, but also find someone in your community who is a successful communications person and make them your new best friend. And, of course, read the rest of this book to help you get a better handle on more ways to make your library relevant for the next generation.

**MOXIE TIP**  If you are feeling overwhelmed by the extent of what you are expected to be doing, consider going back to the basics first. Get your website in order before you worry about social media. Have an effective email marketing program in place with a steadily growing list before you jump into video or slide sharing. These two things along with the addition of a blog should be the hub of all of your other marketing efforts. Everything else that you do should drive your customers back to these top three channels—your website, blog, and eNewsletters.

The use of branding, a mission, and a vision need to be in place for one big reason: fulfilled positive promises make good library supporters. And what would a library be without supporters? To reach this promise, your library must have several items in place. First, a brand is a promise of an experience, period. So you need to make sure you and your staff know what you are promising before you can try to communicate it to others. Having your mission and vision messages ready and available add to your brand. Next, a professionally created logo will be the cornerstone of presenting your promise to your supporters. To be sure that your brand is being conveyed properly to your supporters, a communications audit is a necessary step. Finally, understanding where people are interacting with your brand, why they are using the communications channel, and why it is resonating with them is essential to creating an effective marketing plan. A well-thought-out plan will show why your library matters. Content, timing, and communication channels are serious factors that lead to targeted brand exposure. Surveys, focus groups, and metrics are all tools you can use to attain your goals. Getting your library in order takes a lot of steps, so break down the process into smaller steps and just remember your goal: fulfilling your promise to create good library customers and supporters!

## REFERENCE

Newman, D. (2013). *Do It! Marketing*. Chicago: American Management Association.

# 2

# EVERYONE IS IN MARKETING

## STAFF EMPOWERMENT

In a world where job titles, job descriptions, and silo mentality reign, one of the hardest things to do is to convince others that marketing and promotion are part of everyone's job. You can do everything possible to get people to come into the library for a program or service, but if they do and the staff person they speak with doesn't know anything about it or gives off negative vibes, you have failed. Most libraries, whether big or small, are bound by distinct job titles for their employees. Depending on the culture of the organization, these titles fit into the extremes of "we're all in this together to serve the public" attitude or the "my job is more important than your job" attitude. The majority of organizations tend to come in somewhere in between these two viewpoints. For the purposes of this book, the term *staff* refers to every staff person, from the part-time shelver and the security staff to the executive director.

The job of the communications and marketing person often entails serving the internal audience of the library also. If this is the case at your library, the best way to proceed is to look at them just as you would your external audience. Begin by knowing your organization's personality and the image they portray to the public or brand promise they are sharing. Undertake the following steps to put together an internal marketing plan:

- Know what staff thinks and wants
- Understand what image they are projecting
- Know what your goals and objectives are
- Develop clear key messages
- Develop and promote organizational identity among staff
- Use staff as marketing deputies in each facility

### What Does Your Staff Think?

Judging what the staff thinks can be hard for a new communications person. When I was new to my job, I was sometimes confronted with hostility that I couldn't tell where it was coming from. As I began to learn the culture, I also learned the "who is really in charge" scenario for each of our facilities and made it a goal to seek out those staff members and befriend them. Having someone who is in tune with staff interests to call on is imperative to your internal marketing objectives. You can use all of the normal channels to help with learning about what your staff thinks and wants. Complete an internal communications audit, just as you would do for your external customers. Do surveys, have focus groups, use secret shoppers, have contests, and listen to the chatter around the coffee pot. Use any way you can to let them know that you are interested in learning what they think and know. It is especially difficult for a marketing person with a nonlibrary background to figure out the organizational culture, but whether or not that is the case for you, hang in there. Often, the librarians who are the hardest to work with are also the ones who are most passionate about their jobs and, of course, the future of keeping libraries relevant!

**MOXIE TIP** According to Bill Gates, "Your most unhappy customers are your greatest source of learning." This is also true of staff members. Marketing is a team sport, and everyone has a role to play.

### What Image Is Your Staff Projecting?

This is a great opportunity for doing a secret shopper–type campaign. Many retail stores use these techniques all the time to evaluate procedures. If you don't have the money to hire a professional secret shopper firm, try the local college marketing or sociology department and see if they are interested in doing a study. Or gather up a few trusted members of the community and ask them to perform the study. You can do research on how to do a statistically valid study, but really, you are just doing this for a snapshot to see if your libraries' actions match their promise.

### What Are Your Goals and Objectives for Internal Communications?

Like any good goal setting, they should be SMART—as in *SMART Goals* or criteria. Versions of this acronym have been used by various management professionals, such as Ken Blanchard, who uses it in his book *Leadership and the One Minute Manager* (1985), and over the years have been modified by other business trendsetters. Even though this system has been around for quite a while, it is broad enough that you can use it with business goals, education goals, and even personal goals; but if you are unfamiliar with it, here is the short version to get you started, as explained by George Doran (1981).

*S*imple or Specific: Goals should be written simply and should clearly define what you are going to do or what area you are going to improve.

- Who: Who is involved
- What: What will be accomplished by attaining this goal
- Where: Identify a location
- When: Establish a specific timeframe to keep you on task
- Why: What are the benefits of accomplishing this goal

*M*easurable: Goals should be measurable so that you can track your progress toward this goal as well as confirm that you have accomplished the goal. How will you measure whether or not the goal has been accomplished or performed?

*A*chievable: Is the goal possible for you to achieve? Have others been able to successfully achieve it? Do you have the necessary knowledge, skills, abilities, and resources to accomplish the goal? Is there any other type of support that you will need to accomplish it?

*R*ealistic or Results-focused: Can you measure the outcomes of your goal? Outcomes are not the steps it takes to accomplish the goal, but rather, the benefit or purpose of the goal.

*T*imely: Link your goals to a deadline. Having a timeline for accomplishment will create a sense of urgency to accomplish them. This deadline will help make the goal part of your daily to-do list.

## What Are Your Key Messages?

Let the staff know and be involved in messages that are sent out to the public. You can help by giving them business cards with key promotions of the week on them, or by putting up posters in the staff bathroom stalls. Provide a way for them to give you feedback on whether the promotion goals are working or not, as well as if they have better ideas on how to get the word out. Let them help you walk the talk by providing backup to the words with action, helping to make the library brand what your external customers expect.

One of your library's key messages should be that customers come first. The staff needs management support to help them understand the importance of knowing about library services as well as programs and events or special initiatives. Make sure the staff is empowered to solve problems on the spot. Being able to make independent decisions not only shows they are trusted, but it also builds their interest in what is going on at the library, so they will know how to answer questions or to react. On the other hand, if they know that every question asked needs to be handed off to a "more qualified" individual, they will not have the motivation to be as sensitive to customer needs or to the library's inner workings beyond their specific job responsibilities, which certainly applies to any promotional campaigns that may be going on.

Staff members who collaborate with each other and with you will be better able to help achieve your goals and give you feedback on what went well and what didn't. Marketing can also help build that positive culture of cooperation. Some ideas are:

- Hold contests and reward staff members who can sign up the largest number of summer reading participants, or give out the most information cards with your social media information on them.
- Make sure every staff person has a Hawaiian shirt to wear for "Tropical Week."
- Hold a banned-books decorating/display contest between branches and have your customers vote on which one they like the most.
- Ask staff to hand out "$2 Fine Free Cards" to individuals who are over a certain number on the holds list.
- Allow staff to waive or reduce extended-use fees.
- Have them enter customers into a drawing if they sign up for your email newsletter.
- Ask your staff how they like to be rewarded and what promotional ideas they might have.

## DEVELOPING ORGANIZATIONAL IDENTITY

Add to the heading above the word "positive." All organizations have an identity; your job is to make sure that your library's identity is shared system wide, as well as to have it seen in a positive way to both your staff and your external customers. Many multibranch library systems take on the identity of the location and customers they serve, which is the way it should be. What I am referring to here is a systemic identity of shared brand, in that even if customers go into a library across town from their local library, they feel as welcomed and as at home in the new library as the one they usually go to. Policies and procedures should be the same, signage wording should be the same, and so on.

This leads us to visual identity as it pertains to staff. Does your staff have professional looking name tags; do you supply them with smocks, or logoed T-shirts? When a patron walks into the library, can they tell who the staff people are? Can they tell by the signage where to check something out or ask a question? Do you have a dress code? All of these types of questions lead to development of an organizational identity.

## STAFF AS YOUR MARKETING DEPUTIES

Through the process of an internal communications and brand audit, you will likely become familiar with who among the staff can become a marketing deputy. They are normally the ones who ask many questions, want to understand the details, and see change as a welcome concept. These people can help you gain credibility with the rest of the staff and will act as a catalyst for engagement on setting communication standards and mentoring new staff.

Unfortunately, many library employees believe that their sole purpose is to help customers on a transactional basis. Libraries track data such as how many people a day ask for directions, how many ask where to find a book, how many have research or media questions—the list goes on and on. Of course, this data tracking is worthwhile when looking at staffing, facility organization, and other issues, but while you go about these one-on-one interactions, what are you really learning about your customers? How can you take all of this information and expand the role of the staff to include gaining valuable insights that you can use in your marketing efforts? Staff members are sometimes reluctant to take the extra step when consulting with a customer to ask them if they would like to sign up for your eNewsletter or friend your library on Facebook. Because of this, the communications manager works in a vacuum of pumping out information day after day that doesn't always flow down to the people you are trying to reach.

Recently, when our volunteer coordinator retired, I was faced with putting together a special event where I needed numerous volunteers. I went to the staff in the children's area at each location and asked who their most enthusiastic volunteer was. Staff responded with numerous names, and when I told them all about the special event that was being planned, they got even more excited about which of their wonderful volunteers they thought would be the perfect fit. This is relationship building at the highest level, and the staff got excited not only about the prospects of their favorite volunteer being asked to help at the event, but also about the event itself, which normally might not have happened until they read about it in the newsletter or saw the poster.

This interaction helped me understand a few basic things.

- People respond better when they feel a personal stake in the outcome.
- People respond better when asked to do one specific thing.
- The volunteer coordinator had left with all of the organizational memory of 20 years of volunteer relationships that should have been saved somehow—hmmm, I digress; that is a topic for another book.

In the past, I would have used the volunteer coordinator to find the volunteers, and I would have missed the special organizational and personal knowledge that the staff would have had on who would be the best fit. These staff people have now shown me that they can be counted on as marketing deputies.

## STAFF ENGAGEMENT AND INTERNAL COMMUNICATION

As part of your internal communications audit, ask the staff how they like to get their information. Do they prefer email, do they want flyers in the break room, or do they prefer having their manager tell them information at morning meetings? Chances are, just as with your external audiences, it will be a mixed bag of everything. To address this, our system has put into effect the following internal communication channels.

- An internal intranet where information can go out to staff, along with a "Kudos" feature where anyone can add a message of congratulations or thanks about another staff member.
- A staff Facebook group page that is closed to the public.
- Morning meetings, where the staff gathers for 5 to 10 minutes at the beginning of the day in each facility to get information.
- Quarterly all-staff meetings. We use these meetings to give staff a heads-up on anything important that is coming up—website redesign, summer reading changes, changes in benefits.
- General all-staff email blasts.
- A private internal social network, such as Yammer (http://www.yammer.com), could be used to help expand the free flow of information.

Some organizations produce an internal staff newsletter as well as use other technologies to keep staff informed such as voicemail alerts. Figure out what your staff responds to best and do it, even if it may cost a little more to pay people for an extra 15 minutes of time, or to print off a "Top Five Things for This Week" list. Bottom line is, if the staff doesn't know about your efforts, they can't help you.

Staff engagement means customer engagement. How can staff help you accomplish your marketing goals though their daily touch points with customers? Do you have a way to track how your customers' needs are met and the effects of that interaction? If you have a service in which patrons can ask for reading recommendations either by phone or email, how often does a staff member follow up with that customer in six months' time to see if they were happy with the suggestions or had any more questions, or that the staff member remembered they liked Westerns and the library is holding a Western-themed program?

These are the relationship-building acts that go farther than any other amount of marketing you can do. Training staff to see that they are really the marketers is a tough job, but the efforts will pay off!

---

**Ideas to Help Your Staff Become Marketing Deputies:**

- Encourage and challenge staff to amaze at least half of their customers every day about their knowledge outside the library walls (use your secret shopper for this one). Have your secret shopper ask about community event information that is happening outside the library, or about where to find community resources not associated with the library. If your staff adopts a customer-centric mind-set, they should broaden their knowledge base to what is important to your customers, as well as library information.
- Hire staff who have a passion for helping people. Sounds like a no-brainer, but consider those peers who make you wonder why they ever got into this field.
- Track those interactions that you can follow up on, even if it is just an email saying, "Thanks for coming into the library today."
- Get staff to brainstorm their customer service strengths to give not only good customer service, but amazing service.
- Ask staff to be transparent about their library love—what they read, who their favorite author is, what their history with libraries is—and use this information for blogs, newsletters, and social media.
- Have a feedback loop for one-to-one interactions. This could be a form that the customer fills out, or a three-question email survey. These should be used for good and not-so-good interactions.

---

## WORD OF MOUTH MARKETING (WOMM)

Word of mouth marketing as defined by Andy Sernovitz (2006) is "Everything you can do to get people talking." It is your job (and the staff's job) to get people talking about the good things at the library. Something wonderful and WOMM-worthy probably happens in your library every day. The hard part is getting the staff to tell you about it and being able to use it!

A WOMM strategy should be added into your library marketing plan. The frontline staff is your most valuable asset in making this happen. If each one of your staff members tells 10 people every day about your new homework help database, and those 10 people tell 10 of their friends, and so on, you can see how this would work toward achieving the marketing goals.

People love to spread good news (and bad) about the library. All you need to do is find a way to listen to what is being said, capture it, and figure out how to use it. Do a search on social media sites for your library's name or hashtag. I once found in the personal section of Craigslist a scathing complaint from a person who had to pay for a lost book. Our policy is to say something positive about using the library when we come across these types of comments, so as to not get into a comment war with an anonymous customer. If you find good posts, share them to make them go farther.

Do you have comment or suggestion boxes in your library? Make sure those ideas are forwarded to you along with the person who needs to respond. Your staff should all have your email or contact information to hand out to people interested in talking about library services, an experience they had, or a program idea they have. Our library district is fortunate to have an Answer Center (call center) staffed with very knowledgeable folks who answer all the phone calls. They constantly refer to me conversations that they have with our customers that they feel should either be saved or followed up with.

I recently had an unplanned WOMM event when the filter on our email providers system failed and 87,000 emails went out to the wrong people! After going through the over 1,000 replies of people confused, worried they had been hacked, and other various questions, the next day we sent out an apology note with the reasons why they had gotten the wrong email. I assumed that would be about all I would see, but because my name was on the apology email, I got hundreds of replies from people with very kind words. Quotes like "While I got this email in error, it did serve to remind me about all the resources you have. So I just signed up for your newsletter and look forward to your weekly updates." Or, "No problem. The Library District is still our favorite institution, and especially the people that work there. You're the best! If other institutions, both public and private, were as well-run, responsive, helpful, transparent, and accountable as you, this would be paradise!" Or, "No worries, thanks for handling it all so responsibly, we love the library and the wonderful environment you provide every day. Thank you!" WOW! Then the newspaper ran a brief saying that it was a system malfunction and not to worry, people stopped me in the grocery store when I was wearing my name tag and asked me about it, friends and family called me about it, and on and on.

After the initial shock of this happening, I went into crisis management mode and started going through my crisis checklist. I wrote a message and emailed it out to all of our staff so that if they received questions, they had the correct response. I hoped to turn it around to be a positive, by personally thanking each person who had written or called in asking about the glitch; they were instrumental in helping us test our system that had obviously failed, as well as sending the apology out through all our social media channels, and I was rewarded in return. Talk about word of mouth! I got enough comments to fill up three pages of paper, and now we are working on doing a program on cyber security. They talked, and we listened.

Try out a WOMM campaign—they really are fun, if you can plan for them ahead of time!

- Find your big idea—a clear, compelling message
- Add it as a strategy to your marketing plan
- Let the staff (and volunteers) know how to deliver that message and the importance
- Find a way to collect the testimonials or success stories
- Ask staff to help you collect the good and the bad

WOMM campaigns can be big or small; you just need to give people something to talk about that they will want to share. It might be a surprise door prize for the 10th customer for a week, or a new service of books delivered by bicycle. Enlist everyone to help by giving people a button to wear with a bicycle on it, or by putting up displays in the library that are conversation starters. The most important thing to remember about WOMM is that it should be fun. It's not what you say, but the passion with which you say it that will get others talking. Check out WordofMouth.org (http://www.wordofmouth.org) for checklists, worksheets, and more.

Nurture your library staff as a group of big idea people and grand thinkers. Publish their ideas as visible experts in your social media and on your blog. Have them do a presentation for your slide-sharing site or for a webinar or podcast. Using the reputation of the knowledgeable *librarian* will help you gain credibility in the eyes of your customer about the importance of the library in the world of Google.

Your new job description is to serve your internal audience. Creating a successful marketing plan and brand means having *everyone's* buy in. No plan can be successful if your staff is not projecting your brand to the public. To help this process, an internal marketing plan can be put in place. Understanding the culture of your organization will make your life easier. Set some SMART goals as you create an organizational identity. Remember, your staff members are your marketing deputies. They are in the trenches each day and can be one of your best assets to understanding your supporters. Get them talking!

## REFERENCES

Blanchard, K. (1985). *Leadership and the One Minute Manager.* New York: William Morrow & Company.

Doran, G. T. (1981). "There's a S.M.A.R.T. Way to Write Management's Goals and Objectives." *Management Review* (AMA FORUM) 70(11): 35–36.

Sernovitz, A. (2006). *Word-of-Mouth Marketing: How Smart Companies Get People Talking.* Chicago: Kaplan Publishing.

# 3

# PROMOTING EVENTS AND PROGRAMS

## WALK THE TALK

As a library marketer, you are always on call to be in the know. If you are being asked to get the word out to the community and staff, than you need to make sure that you are receiving the information that you need. If your library has a management structure in which a supervisor feeds you information, be sure to set up a clear channel of communication in both directions so that at a minute's notice—for example, when the newspaper editor calls to ask about an event—you will know the answer.

One of the hardest jobs in the library is that of event programmer. It can also be the most creative and rewarding. It is our job as library marketers to get people into the library for these wonderful programs. If you are from a small library, you may be the marketer and the programmer. Good for you! In many ways this is easier than working with a separate group to make sure that the vision that you have for the program is seen by the community. On the other hand, when you are waist-deep in cutting out stars for the craft program or pulling together all the robot components for your maker space program, the last thing you want to think about is the marketing.

Whether or not you have a role beyond marketing, there are some simple concepts you should be aware of, and some basic things you should do.

### Who Is the Program Designed For?

If you are the person in charge of program promotion, hooray! You can bring all of your creativity and enthusiasm together to make the program successful. Promotion of library programs can be as easy or as complicated as the program itself. You can spend hours working up a marketing plan, spend just an hour brainstorming and using a template you already have, or fly by the seat of your pants and throw it out there into the universe and see where it sticks. Something in between the second and third ideas is usually the most practical approach—yes, really! As much as you would like to do marketing plans for everything that comes across your desk, realistically, you probably don't have the time. That said, to keep you on track, there should always be an overall plan in place that includes your programs in general for the year.

In marketing school we learned about target audiences; now, the better and better-defined term is audience segmentation. The person setting up the program needs to answer the question: Who is this program designed for? After you know who you are reaching out to, your target audience, you can use these steps to add the event into your content calendar and make it a success.

**Step 1: Program title and description.** Picking the right name and description for a program is crucial. Staff members often tend to use words like "literacy" or "educational" in their program descriptions. While using these sorts of words in your description make you sound like you are fulfilling the mission of the library, your customers tend to want something from you that is more like entertainment, with some learning thrown in. Kids and teens especially aren't interested in going to something educational after they have been to school all day. Save those descriptors for the program objectives statement and internal information. Change titles from "Learn How to Knit" to "My Sister Knits and So Can You!" or "Learn How to Use Microsoft Word" to "Send Out Professional Letters." Here are a few power words to help you brainstorm:

- Bold, Delightful, Dynamic, Electrifying, Inspirational, Intense, Hysterical, Gusty, Brave, Artistic, Courageous, and Loyal.
- Check out "317 Power Words That'll Instantly Make You a Better Writer" by Jon Morrow at *Boost Blog Traffic* (http://www.boostblogtraffic.com/power-words).

Work with the programmer to brainstorm names and edit the copy to justify the time spent on doing the promotions for the program, and to ensure that people will come!

Another issue to consider is the use of gender-neutral words. In this age of politically correct journalistic speak, we tend to be overly concerned about making sure we are using terminology correctly. Sometimes, in order to reach new audiences, you need to become a little stereotypical. Instead of a class titled "Learn to Eat Healthy," call it "Why Men Love Bacon." Grab their attention and then make it sound like something they really should come to. If your program title doesn't sound typical for a library event, then you are on the right track. Use the Twitter test for your program descriptions. Try to describe the gist of the main program information in 140 characters. If you can't do that, how are you going to promote it through your social media channels?

Some sample ideas for program titles might include:

- *Learn to Paint* might be changed to *Cocoa and Canvas*: "*Have you always wanted to paint with oils? Learn the basics from painter Missy McGee. Free, no registration, 7 PM, Main Library 11/14 for more info:* [link to library webpage calendar]." This program can be cross promoted in the art as well as the food areas of your library!
- *Learn to Knit* might be changed to *Madame Rene's Knitting Salon*: "*Did you know knitting salons have a historical significance in our town? Beginning knitters this class is for you! Madame Rene will start with the basics for this weekly event. Free. Registration required. Your*

*Library 1/16 4–5 PM for more info:* [link to library webpage calendar]." Class could be cross promoted by a local yarn shop as well as the local historical society!

- *Tech Assistance for Women* could be *Tech Goddess Service:* "*You can be a tech goddess! Hands-on class for women who want to do their own computer maintenance, no more asking for help! Free, no registration, 7 PM, Main Library 9/10 for more info:* [link to library webpage calendar]." This can be cross promoted by your website as well as a local women's center!

As a library marketer, you need to be empowered to revise copy and curate or even over-rule images given to you. As they say, a picture is worth a thousand words; by using photos along with great graphic design for your promotions, you can grab people's attention. Have your staff take high-quality photos (300 dpi or higher) at your events for promotional use. Many phones have an automatic setup to downsize photos so that they can be sent faster through email or social media. You may need to set up a brown-bag-lunch tutorial for staff who take program photos about the best way to take and save photos, especially if they use phones or tablets to take them. Get them involved in the promotion; everyone likes to take pictures! Set up a shared folder on your computer network where staff can upload the photos for future use. (See Chapter 9 on setting up a shared marketing cache.)

Have your photo permission policy in place. Some libraries hand out actual photo permission slips and have the customers sign them, especially if a program features lots of children. Keeping track of all of the signed slips is a bookkeeping nightmare. This was more of a standard when people didn't have cameras in their phones. With the advent of a social media photo-taking culture, more libraries have a sign posted in the meeting or storytime rooms that states something like, "Photos may be taken for Library promotional use. If you do not want your picture taken, please let the staff member know." An announcement is made at the beginning of the program, and anyone not wanting to be in photos can raise their hands or move to a certain area of the room. Library privacy policy is a tricky business, and even though a photography statement may be announced during a program, if you are taking photos of people at the computer lab or browsing for books, you may still need to have them sign a release form, especially if it is a parent signing for their child. Whatever your library decides is appropriate through your legal channels should be posted in the building and written up and sent out to staff so everyone knows what the policy and procedures are for photography inside your buildings.

**Step 2: Word of Mouth Marketing (WOMM).** What person in your community knows the most about the people who would likely come to the program or event? For example, if you are having a tribute to World War II veterans program, it might be the executive director at the veterans' center. Call that person and tell him or her about the program. They will likely have insights to share, like "Don't do the program at 7 PM, because the WWII vets won't come out that late," or "Make sure you have cookies." You can share these details with the programmer. Also when looking for key communicators for your WOMM marketing campaign, be sure to include all library staff members. After all, they are the frontline marketers with your community.

**Step 3: High-tech Media Campaign.** Plan your email blasts and blog posts, and schedule the posting of the event on your social media channels. This sounds easy, but it can be a tricky business. There are marketing people on both sides of the aisle on whether you should use a social media content scheduling and dashboard tool, such as TweetDeck (http://www .tweetdeck.com), Hootsuite (http://www.hootsuite.com), or CoSchedule (http://www .coschedule.com). These scheduling tools can give you a one-stop place to add in updates to all (or most of) your social media channels. If you are scheduling content and monitoring many channels, being able to see where and what will be going out live in one place makes it easier to make sure you haven't missed anything as well as to change updates fast if a program is cancelled or a time changed. They also let you see how your hashtags are being used, as well as if anyone has sent you a direct message or mentioned you in a social media post. Some marketers, like Heather Mansfield (2012), claim that your social media reach goes down by using one of these dashboard systems, because you lose touch of how your followers are experiencing the individual sites, and it is too easy to just automate your messaging without remembering who you are messaging to. I usually do a combination of both scheduling techniques. I use a scheduling dashboard that helps me lay out my content so I can see it at a glance, but I also periodically check the channels to see if any trends are happening that I want to tag on to, or if one of my channels has been going down in my stats; if so, I will pay special attention to it and try to raise the engagement numbers.

Each social media channel has a unique community that you need to remember when developing your content. It has also been mentioned that the ways the different social media channels set up their algorithms may also interfere with using a scheduling dashboard—for example, Facebook status updates are not sent out to as many of your friends if sent through a third-party system. Having worked with and without a dashboard system, the biggest concern that I have found is that without one, each of your social media feeds shows the content slightly differently. So, if you only have a few minutes a day to work on social media, using an aggregator tool may be the best choice. It is certainly better than not posting anything, and letting your channel die.

**MOXIE TIP**

Even if for some reason your library isn't yet working with social media, you need to make sure you go beyond the press release.

- Add the event to other organizations' social media and website calendars.
- Ask if you can be a guest blogger for the local events blogger in your town.
- Look for Meetup groups (http://www.meetup.com) in your area that have a focus on the event subject area (i.e., Travel Meetups for a program about Iran).
- Reach out to local schools, day-care centers, homeschool organizations, or neighborhood HOAs to get on their social media feeds.
- Have an internal staff Facebook page so you can ask staff to share out library information on their own feeds.

**Step 4: High-Touch Media Campaign.** Flyers, bookmarks, posters, notices printed on the bottom of the date-due slips, scrolling type at the bottom of the screens of television monitors, graphics on the public computer monitors—these can all be considered "high-touch" media. Of course, there are almost endless ways you can reach your potential audience with these methods, and that can be overwhelming; but think simply first (break it down into little chunks), and start there. One way to start might be to put together a template for bookmarks that go to children; these would carry your library's image and brand standards along with an image that might be used in your children's area. The specific event information could be dropped into the setup, and then the final could be sent to the library branches for them to print, cut, and distribute. Volunteers are especially welcome for these types of in-house printing and distribution.

Using an online event calendar system can save you a lot of headaches. Our library system is comprised of three buildings, with numerous rooms to reserve for library programs as well as for public use. The online calendar system many library systems use is called Evanced (http://www.evancedsolutions.com), which helps with room reservations also. If you work with a city government, you may have access to a calendaring system through the recreation department or your special events venue. Even though where I work is a relatively small system, we host up to 60 programs a month. One of the hardest things about conducting effective marketing and promotion campaigns is making sure you have information about the content of the programs early. We follow a procedure in which the programmers add their program information directly into our online calendar at least two months in advance (and for summer reading programs, it is six months in advance). The information is then pulled from that source and used for the printed monthly calendar, posters, social media posts, weekly email updates, and website features. Any changes to a program require updating the online calendar first with an email to me. This way we always know that the go-to place for correct information is the online calendar. If there is any question about a program, staff can check the calendar for the most current information. And the library can make sure they have the rooms booked before they are released to the public for booking. Some months, you may have additions of events, for example, if an author comes into town unexpectedly; but overall, getting staff to think way ahead has been the best way to plan and market your events.

## GETTING MEDIA ATTENTION

The most important question to ask yourself when determining whether this program will get media attention is: Is it news? Some small print media outlets such as small local newspapers are constantly looking for news items to put in their paper, and they will gobble up anything you send them. Many small-town papers even give the library a weekly or monthly column to tell their story; this can be the greatest asset small libraries have. After all, everyone wants to find something to do, and folks in small towns are more likely to see their local library as a vital community center. However, larger media outlets with daily papers are more likely to fill their local sections with what they see as more newsworthy stories.

What often works well in landing your story in these larger media outlets is offering photographic opportunities. Pitch your story to the paper's photographers as well as to the local news journalist, so they are informed on how many cute, smiling kids will be there for your finger-painting program. Photographers are often eager to come to the events, but advanced coverage is more challenging. Of course, every media market is different, but they all still want to sell papers; so it gets back to, is it news? Does anyone care? If your programming staff is upset because their fabulous idea didn't get on the front page of the paper and they assume that is why no one came, direct the staff to all of the other ways that the information about the program was dispersed; and show that there might have been other reasons why the attendance was low.

Print newspapers and television are still widely considered to be the most important media to gain attention from. An important aspect of your job as a library marketer is to know the contacts at the paper and TV station, and to build relationships with them. If you have media contacts that you have standing relationships with, you are fortunate. Then, you can call them occasionally when you need a favor, and know they will do their best to accommodate your story.

Besides the regular print and TV media people, make connections with local bloggers and other local social media celebrities who can repost your announcements for you to advance your information presence on the Internet. However, before sending them a post, ask yourself, "So what?" If you don't have the answer for them on the so-what question, their followers might not care, and your connections may not want to post it. Adding photos to your press release from last year's event is always helpful, especially for online channels who are always looking for visual content. You can gain credibility with the posts you send by adding great branded photos or visuals for them to use.

Getting media attention boils down to these tasks:

- Build a relationship with the local media journalists and social media gurus
- Ask them how they prefer press releases or announcements be sent to them and how much lead time they need
- Think through any great photo idea pitches that might entice a photographer
- Ask yourself, is it news? Does anyone care and so what? or
- Do something out of the library box that they can't resist covering

**MOXIE TIP**

**Out-of-the-Library-Box Ideas for Gaining Media Attention May Include:**

- Have a speed-dating event at the library and ask the single journalists to participate.
- Have your circulation staff put an informational bookmark into every book they check out.
- Use a teen volunteer to stand outside the library with one of those twirling signs.
- March with a sandwich board through your downtown, giving out ice cream samples.
- Hold a dog-walkers' protest brigade, having them march with library signs.
- If you can't get coverage in the regular sections of the paper, send a letter to the opinion section.
- Hold a pre-event to focus media attention on the real event, so you don't get only day-of coverage. For instance, if you are holding an event with a panel discussion on global warming, you may ask the mayor of your town to plant a tree at one of your facilities the week before. The mayor would be newsworthy, and then you can have the media plug the upcoming event.
- Tie the program into a trending topic in your town. For example, if everyone is complaining about the heat, you can have a cool-off at your library series.
- Send the journalists coffee and donuts. Remember, print media people are on a different schedule than most nine-to-five types. Find out the schedule and show up at the paper with snacks late at night when they need a break.

## PROGRAM FEEDBACK

One of the most overlooked steps in marketing library programs is getting customer feedback and evaluating how successful they were. Using various ways to gain feedback not only helps you run better programs, it also helps you with your audience segmentation and marketing plans. One of the best ways to get feedback is to hand out a form with no more than three questions at the beginning of the program, and then pick them up when it is over. The program host mentions it in the introduction and asks for the optional response from the participants. You can vary the form a bit, depending on what type of program it is, and design the form with checkboxes (most people don't like to write a long response unless they have very strong feelings one way or another), a one-to-five rating scale for the program/presenter, and a scale for a question about impact, such as "Did you learn something that will improve an aspect of your life?" Include checkboxes for how they learned about the program (media channels) and a space for their optional name and email address to sign up for the weekly email updates. You may not want to use these at every program, but try to do them consistently for a week of programs four times a year to help evaluate not only how the programs are being perceived, but also how people found out about them. You can also build your in-house mailing list for promoting future library programs. (See the Sample Program Feedback Form in the Appendix.)

Some additional high-tech ways in which people are gaining program feedback are through the new *clicker* technologies, where each participant is handed a clicker wand and is asked to say yes or no to a series of questions put up on a screen. This technology is being used quite a bit in educational settings to get an automatic response to see if the students are understanding the information being presented. It has been so successful that companies such as Turning Technologies (http://www.turningtechnologies.com) and iClicker (http://www.iclicker.com) are now coming out with virtual clickers. In other words, you can download an app to your phone or mobile device that will enable it to respond to interactive questions such as multiple choice and short answers given by the facilitator. Another version of this type of questioning system includes the Poll Everywhere (http://www.polleverywhere.com) text-message polling or voting system, which has free and non-profit plans available. This system lets you gain live audience participation by asking them a question on screen using the Poll Everywhere app, then the audience is asked to answer the question using a mobile phone with text capabilities, their Twitter account, or a web browser. You will see the responses live on the screen within seconds. This is especially fun at staff meetings to check to see that staff are listening to the information being presented, as well as use this technique to gain information at the beginning or end of a storytime where caregivers are trying to corral their toddlers.

Make sure you know what is happening in your libraries. This simple idea will make a world of difference in event promotion and programs. Four steps help to create a well-rounded marketing plan for library events:

Step 1: Program title and description
Step 2: Word of Mouth Marketing (WOMM)
Step 3: High-tech media campaign
Step 4: High-touch media campaign

Continued communication with staff is important throughout these steps. Getting media attention not only means traditional sources like the newspaper, but also local bloggers and smaller community newsletters, always ask "So what?" You finally have to evaluate how the event went and get customer feedback. While this can be often overlooked, it is imperative to learn the good and bad so that both programs and marketing for that program get better!

## REFERENCE

Mansfield, H. (2012). *Social Media for Social Good: A How-To Guide for Nonprofits* (p. 51). New York: McGraw-Hill.

# 4

# NEW TWISTS ON TRADITIONAL TECHNIQUES

## POSTERS, HANDOUTS, AND SIGNAGE

With the current emphasis on the new electronic ways to market the library through social media and online, it's easy to overlook the basics. In fact, there are still many benefits to having artfully designed posters and spectacular, easy-to-use signage. For those of you who have professional graphic artists on staff, hooray! The consistent look and feel of professionally done posters, whether printed or done digitally and displayed on a monitor, always go a long way in promoting your library image and brand, gaining attention by the public and helping to tell your library story. If you are a small library that cannot afford a professional artist, use professionally designed templates. When you set up your logo graphic standards as discussed in Chapter 1, be sure to add in a poster template to be used, designed by the same artist who designed the logo. These templates can be saved in a shared file in your marketing language cache of shared marketing reference files (see Chapter 9) with directions for use so that any library staff member can open them and add specific program information to them. Train staff on using the templates and give them the "Who, What, Where, Why and How" message on copywriting and proofreading.

> **MOXIE TIP** Take advantage of your vendors! Many library vendors provide printed or online marketing materials such as posters and bookmarks. Some even give you templates so you can add in your own images and logo. You are already paying them for these items through their contracts, so take advantage. Some even have customer help videos you can add to your YouTube channel. It is to their advantage to have people use their products to keep libraries renewing the contract, so don't be hesitant!

If you do use posters, you can get the most bang for your buck by repurposing your posters in your social media postings, online newsletters, web graphics, and Pinterest boards. The reuse of graphic content is just as important as written content.

Signage is a big part of library marketing that is often overlooked. Do you walk into your library and immediately get hit with rule-based signage like: "NO DRINKS," "NO FOOD," "NO DOGS," etc.? These *rule* signs are so prevalent in some libraries that the signage that you really want your customers to see, like the *Just Out* book display or the restroom signs, can be totally overlooked. Train the library manager on the branding and marketing of her or his library. The library manager should be the only person that can put up a sign. (Unless it is an emergency short-term sign such as "The copier is down," which can also be done by staff from a sign template located on a shared computer drive.)

One of the most beneficial things to do when you start your library's marketing makeover is to conduct a signage audit. Go through the building and remove every sign; then have staff keep track of what questions they are asked for a week. If it comes back that people are asking more than three times in a week where the public phone is, then you can have that sign updated with the graphic standards in place and put back up. If the questions aren't asked, leave the sign down—less sensory overload for library visitors.

There's a lot we can learn about signage from the retail world. Corporations spend thousands of dollars studying the way people look at their signage and move through a store; and there are specific reasons why particular items are placed near the checkout or in the furthest corner of the store. Many of the insights found in the retail world can be used in the library world, and if you take heed, your customers will thank you. Signage is one of the transferable products that marketers can use. Go into your local department stores and take pictures of the signs. Take the photos back to the library, print them out, and study them. How big is the type size? What colors and fonts do they use? Are they hung from the ceiling, or put on stands? Are they general, or specific? Take the information gained from your signage audit and see how you might incorporate some of these retail ideas into your library.

One of the best new products on the market is vinyl lettering that can be rubbed onto a painted wall and then rubbed off when no longer needed. This type of signage is affordable, and you can even add them to a mounted surface, such as foam core board or metal, if you don't want to put them directly on the wall. The benefit is that they are easily moved. If your library is like mine, things are constantly being moved around. Nonfiction and oversized books are shuffled; the graphic novel section keeps expanding. Vinyl lettering can help you keep your signage professional looking and up to date inexpensively.

If you have high ceilings in your library, consider using two-sided hanging banners. Full-color printed banners of various sizes can be ordered from online stores. They are affordable and fast, and they can be used for location signage as well as for special events and initiatives like Summer Reading. Vistaprint (http://www.vistaprint.com) and GotPrint (http://www.gotprint.com) are just two of the sites where you can order affordable banner printing. After your banner campaign is over, reuse and upcycle the banners by having a local sewing company reformat the banners into bags that can be sold in your library or by your Friends of the Library group. People love to have a library souvenir of the event or a one-of-a-kind gift to give, and you can make up for the cost of the banner (and hopefully add more to your marketing budget). If you don't have a lead on a local industrial sewer, ask around at your local farmer's market or visit the nonprofit organization Mission Wear website (http://www.themissionwear.org).

## DISPLAYS

As you are out and about shopping, take photos of impressive displays being done in the retail environment. Examine perfume displays in department stores and other high-end retail displays. Visualize those perfume bottles as books and see where that idea can take you. Manufacturers spend thousands of dollars a year studying buying habits, and you can reuse them for free! Add the photos to your online file of ideas in the cloud using accounts such as Evernote or a secret Pinterest board. These can be filed away and shared with other libraries for future use.

Displays are one of the most effective ways to tell your story, gain attention, boost circulation, and empower your internal library marketers. Don't have room to do face-out book displays? Then do some weeding and get creative!

- Pick a theme (such as gardening)
- Gather your props—gloves, watering can, pots, real or fake plants, bag of potting soil, etc. (No budget or storage space? Ask your local gardening store if you can borrow them for two weeks and in return put out a stack of their business cards on the display.)
- Gather gardening books and media.
- Books will fly off the shelves, so hold a few back to restock, or gather peripheral materials that might fit, such as gardening for exercise or world-famous gardens.
- Hang a banner from the ceiling above the display. If you are short on budget money, hang props from fishing line above or use stands with different heights. Generic seasonal vinyl banners can be custom-designed and produced from online companies and can be used year after year. (Don't forget your logo!)
- Use battery-powered lights or turning stands to get attention in a dark corner.
- Promote the display with a poster at the nursery, and send photos of it through your social media. Alert the local media and visitor's center/Chamber of Commerce.
- Tell the staff about the display, so they can refer to it when speaking with customers.
- Ask staff to wear flowers on their name badges.

Are you planning to do a feature display, but want the books to stay on it? Don't! If you want to put together a display of banned books and would like the public to see all of the titles, put images of the covers on the display, and keep copies of the actual books below. Remember, the point of doing a display is to get the materials in people's hands and out the door.

Plan to keep the display up for two weeks. After that, all the materials should be checked out and the bibliophiles that come in weekly (or daily) have stopped "seeing" it.

**MOXIE TIP** Don't forget to add a "display" schedule as part of your marketing plan, and look for those creative staffers in your system that will take this task on with enthusiasm.

If your goal is to start a conversation with your customers or to engage them in learning about something new, don't shy away from controversial themes for your displays. Have one side of your display be *pro* and one side *con*; giving both sides of the discussion equal space is important to the library staying on neutral ground. For instance, you could have diet and nutrition displays with one display on low-carb, high-fat diets and another display next to it that focuses on high-carb, low-fat diets. Starting out with a display that may have a controversial edge to it may be the best way to gain attention.

Keep track of other community events in your town that can tie in to your materials. We had a national bike race come through town, so we asked the local bike shop to give us jerseys and a bike to display alongside all of our bike-related materials. The jerseys hanging from the ceiling looked like national flags waving and gave a new festive appearance to the lobby as customers walked in. They couldn't help but wonder what was going on, and of course, they looked at the books, too.

Be proud of your displays! Enter library display contests or start one in your state. Are you responsible for more than one library? Than have a contest between libraries and ask your customers to vote online for the one they like best.

## MERCHANDISE

Many libraries that have been able to brand themselves as a destination place (think New York Public Library) or have loyal followings find that having logoed postcards, mugs, or book bags add to their revenue streams. Even if your library does not have that kind of prominence, using merchandise can still be a great way to get your name into the community. Consider selling items such as book bags and logoed jump drives with the library logo; or even better, sell items that go along with your special events or anniversary celebrations.

If you add merchandising into your marketing plan in hopes that everyone you see at the grocery store will be using the library bag to carry their groceries, go ahead and put it in the budget as an expense, and just give out a bag to everyone who walks in the library. Realistically, it is better to think of these types of items in the same way you would hand out bookmarks. If you are trying to sell items, the markup needs to pay for the item as well as shipping, time of staff to restock, and so on, and doesn't leave much room for making a profit. T-shirts can be especially tricky, since it seems you never have the right style, color, or size that the person wants on hand. If you are considering giveaway items that might be used at an event with a booth, try having a spin-wheel where people can spin for the item; that way you can engage them in conversation instead of them just walking by and grabbing a pen off your table without having to talk to you.

**MOXIE TIP** If possible, add a call to action to your giveaway items. Give out a pen with your logo and website on one side and a special "get your questions answered hotline" phone number on the other side, with a special code for tracking. That way you can trace how many calls come in as a result of your efforts. Surround your giveaway booth with question marks and tell people that the 40th caller with a library question will win a special prize. Getting your customers to engage with the library on a personal level, even if it is just to trying to win a prize, helps them to remember you and your message better, rather than having them take a pen and sticking it into their drawer.

If you do decide to sell an item, schedule the theme and sale around an event. Recently, the Elf on a Shelf has been gaining a lot of popularity during the December shopping season. Build off of that with a Worm in the Stacks, where people can buy your Book Worm and take photos of it in various places, and have them post the photos to Facebook or Flickr pages using your library's name in the hashtag. You can give a prize out to the most exotic locale, or do a prize drawing from all the entries. Make it a timed event (such as two weeks or a month) to increase the sense of urgency and "get them while available" type of promotion.

## EVERYONE LOVES A PARADE

Yes, everyone loves a parade, except the people who have to plan it. This falls under the piece of your job description that says "all other duties assigned." I have been through my share of parades and fair booths. Many of these opportunities really are wonderful marketing events (our float even won first place one year), but they need to be well thought out and need to be a part of your overall strategic plan and marketing strategies. If one of the goals of your strategic plan is to address the homework help needs of 'tweens, than maybe having a booth at the Brownie jamboree is a good fit. Be thoughtful and strategic about where you go and why. Your strategy will also give you a rationale for turning down the ones that don't fit. We attended a Senior Fair for many years until we realized that the attendees already knew us, knew how to check out materials, and were not really interested in anything new that we had to offer. So now we just put a flyer into the goodie bag rather than having staff spend time manning a booth.

Getting outside the library walls is a crucial part of the marketing effort. You need to go where your community goes to understand how to market to them. Do you live in a place that has a festival or two every weekend during the summer? Does everyone in your town cycle through the farmer's market on Saturday? If people ride on mass transit in your city, place your posters up front and center to passengers who are staring out the window. If the kids in your community all hang out at the community pool, go there so you can find out where they get their information from.

Anytime that you can do something outside of the library—put up a display, hold an event, put up posters, pass out bookmarks, or have a flash reading mob in your downtown—you gain visibility with the nonlibrary users you are always trying to attract . Whether handing out books at the skateboard park or pedaling the book bicycle around town, just showing up can bring new members into your library. Doing things outside the walls of your building makes people stop and think about that big building full of books that they had forgotten about. It never ceases to amaze me how often I hear "What is the library doing here?" as I'm giving out logoed water bottles during a 5K race or other community activity. People are often pleasantly surprised to see the library out in the community, and that sends a message that the library is part of the community.

Surveys are good for certain things, but hearing firsthand where your community gets their information is priceless. And if you do end up spending a weekend manning a library booth at the Pet Lovers Convention, make sure that it is a win-win for you and for the participants. Gather as much information from them as they are getting from you.

## CONTESTS

People of all ages love contests, and the cooler the prizes, the better turnout you will have. This is where some of your business partnerships can come into play—by asking partners for donations of prizes for the contest. It is amazing who will come out of the woodwork for a contest; they are a great way to engage your community with the library. Besides the annual summer reading coloring contest, ramp up your moxie marketing by holding some out-of-the-box competitions!

- Competitions that focus on *Amazing Race*– or *Survivor*-type team building. This is basically an updated version of a scavenger hunt—teams need to work together to find clues to the next *pit stop*, where they complete different challenges and gather clues to go forward to the next stop. Go to PartyGamesPlus.com (http://www.PartyGamesPlus.com) for ideas and resources.
- Naming the new library mascot.
- Branch-to-branch scavenger hunt completions using QR codes to find the next clue.
- Video competitions—ask people to upload videos to your YouTube channel in accordance with a certain theme or event.
- Photo contests—have people share their photos using a hashtag through their Instagram account.
- Check-ins—Foursquare recently split their functions into Foursquare and Swarm; Swarm has the new check-in capabilities, and Foursquare is more of a geo-locational finder and local search tool. It sounds like this will open up some fun contest opportunities. You can ask your customers to *check-in* through the app when they come into the library, and then you can look through the check-ins and pick a random person to win a prize. Put a time frame on it for a week or two to ramp up people coming through the doors to use their smartphones to check-in.
- Costume contests for cosplay, anime, comics, and superheroes are all great ideas, as well as fun ways to get new and different people engaged in your library.
- Have an avatar swap-off week, perhaps during National Library Week. Ask your library supporters to customize their own social avatars with a special formatted library, which can be downloaded from your website. These avatars will then show up in all of your supporter's social media posts instead of their photo and show their support of the library. There are many tools that you can use to supply people with an avatar overlay, which would lay your library's logo design as a transparency over their own social media photo or avatar. You might check out Twibbon (http://www.twibbon.com) to start a campaign with Twitter and Facebook integration.
- Launch a *Like* contest—set a goal, and the 1,000th person who likes you on Facebook gets a prize.
- Look for great contest ideas that you can adapt to your library through Pinterest. Start a board of ideas to use later.

Some of the social media sites have specific rules regarding contests, so check those out first before you start. They will lock your site or take it down if you are not following the rules.

Contests can be very simple or very complicated, depending on what the submission rules are. Always limit the number of entries people can send in and the amount of information. For example, if you're running a short-story contest, limit the entries to 1,500 words. Think through all of the steps to avoid catastrophes. For one of the poetry contests we held, we ended up with over 300 entries, so we asked staff members to go through the first cut before we handed it over to our judges. That way, our volunteer judges weren't inundated with reading.

But there are also some simpler ways to hold contests that encourage customers to engage with the library. You could host a Facebook chat; at a predetermined time that you have advertised, invite a special guest to log into their individual Facebook account and navigate to the library's Facebook page. A library moderator makes an initial post, such as "It is time to talk to the garden expert"; then participants type their questions into the comment field, and the garden expert responds in the same thread. You could make this a contest by saying the 50th person to comment will get a garden book, a discount coupon for a local nursery, or a special one-on-one meeting with the garden expert.

You could have a similar contest with Twitter by using a special hashtag, or hold a photo-based contest through Instagram. Have people show you what they like most about the library, with a single-line caption telling you about it. All they would have to do is take a photo with their phone, upload it to Instagram, and tag it with the #YourLibraryContest contest hashtag. You can add a page to your website with contest details and rules, and have your web person add the Instagram feed widget code to the web page so everyone can see the photos. You could have your Instagram followers vote for their favorite photo by *likes*, or you could have a committee chose the winning photos. Contests are a great way to engage your communities with the library and what libraries do.

**MOXIE TIP** Remember to include a disclaimer statement that the contestant sees in the rules, stating that anything submitted becomes property of the library. Why? Because the second-most important reason to spend time on contests is to give you content for future annual report quotes and for blog and social media posts, and to create the WOMM buzz in your community. Here is a sample statement that you can have vetted through your legal representatives:

*By submitting an entry, you acknowledge that any contest entries become licensed in perpetuity to the* [Your Library Name] *and its partners via a Creative Commons 3.0 Attribution, Share Alike license* [http://creativecommons.org/licenses/by-sa/3.0].

Whatever contest you decide to hold, write up a step-by-step plan and add in *what if* scenarios, such as, "What if we have 500 kids in the 6-to-10 age category and only 2 in the 10-to-12 age category?" Think it through, then pass it by several staff members to have them weigh in on what questions might be asked, whether they see any pitfalls, etc. Needless to say, the more planning you can put into it, the more successfully and smoothly it will go.

Here are some additional steps to think through while planning a contest:

1. **Why are you running the contest?** What is the goal—are you trying to gain followers for a social media page? Generate more interest in customers signing up for your newsletter? Create specific goals so you will know whether the contest was a success and worth the time.

2. **Pick a relevant prize.** What would motivate people to be interested in the contest and drive them to take the extra step to enter? Do you have community business partners that might

help you with this? What would be a prize relatable to the library that would be relevant to your customers? For our writing contests, along with a cash prize, we also offer to put all of the entries into an eBook to put into our downloadable catalog. So everyone can say they are a published author! Try to think about not just getting as many entries as possible, but making sure that the entries you do get will turn customers into supporters of the library.

3. **Pick an entry method as well as the winning methodology.** Will it be through a social media channel? Through your newsletter, or email system? Through a landing page on your website? Drop off drawing slips at your branches? How will the winner be picked—by random drawing, by judges, etc.?

4. **What information do you want to gain from the contest entry?** Are you going to ask for only name and phone number? Do you need an email address, age, or other demographic information for contact? This goes back to your goals and why you are doing the contest. Gaining information to help with your audience segmentation and, by extension, gaining more contact information should always be one of your priorities for a contest.

5. **Go for it!** To create your contest through a social media channel, investigate others who have used it and determine if there are any stipulations on running a contest. Make your contest visually engaging by prominently featuring photos of your library, the prize, and the name of the contest. Make the entry form easy to read, and have several people look at it and give you feedback. Be sure to include a hashtag so people can share and tweet about the contest.

6. **Deadlines.** Every contest must have an end. It is important to create a sense of urgency not only to drive entries, but to keep it in the foreground of people's minds. Don't run a contest for more than 20 or so days to keep up the urgency. Include a countdown clock on your web page or countdown updates through your social media.

7. **Promotion!** Going back to your contest goals, set up your promotion plan. Post it on your newsfeed, tweet out the contest hashtag and link, print bookmarks and drop them off at stores around town, hang banners in your libraries, post photos of people dropping off their entries on your Instagram and Pinterest pages—whatever you decide is the best way to promote your contest to gain those supporters. Monitor your metrics and analytics to see how people are engaging with the contest. That way you can tweak the content if you need to. Make the promotion so exciting that event people who don't enter will be talking about it and want to know who won.

8. **Pick the winner and follow up with entrants.** Along with just announcing the winner, you may want to blog about them, or feature them on your Facebook page. Send out emails to everyone who entered, thanking them and telling them about the winner. Get them excited about announcing plans for the next contest, creating excitement and generating continued involvement.

The basics of marketing are still your friend! Posters, signs, and handouts can help to create a library system with a consistent brand. You want the inside of your library to match the image that is being given through your marketing and promotions. It is important to not overwhelm your visitors, which you may be doing by providing them with too much information, or by providing them with the wrong information. A signage audit of each branch can help remedy any issues that may be confusing your supporters. And, don't underestimate the power of creating an attractive display to attract your visitors to your materials. Whether you are creating displays, selling merchandise, sponsoring a contest, or joining a parade, make sure that the medium and marketing channels you are using match the attention and participation you are trying to get from visitors.

# 5

# GET SOCIAL WITH YOUR LIBRARY

## SOCIAL MEDIA AND RELATIONSHIP MARKETING

You've probably heard the terms B2B, B2C, ROI, KPI, CRM, and on and on and on—the marketing field is almost as bad as the librarian field for acronyms! A new term coined by Neil Rosen (2012) is "Chatter Marketing." This chatter refers to how customers interact with social media and online businesses. Listening to this chatter and building a one-to-one relationship with your customers is the next wave of marketing. The amount of information collected on each one of us as we go about our daily business is phenomenal. What we say on social media, what we buy, where we are—it goes on and on, not to mention the really personal information such as bank account numbers and credit score! As libraries, we are bound by our laws to keep patron confidentiality as we uphold their freedom to information. We need to walk a fine line when we are looking to use their information to build our relationship with them.

As a library staff member, you are privy to information that tells you a lot about your customers, such as who is pregnant, who is looking to get a divorce, or who is looking for a career change. Especially if you work in a smaller library or in a small town, these people are your neighbors, your waitress at the local café, and the guy at the bank. Building a relationship with these people depends on your discretion about patron privacy—like the Las Vegas tagline, you might say "Whatever is said in the library, stays in the library." So how can you use relationship marketing to your advantage without overstepping that privacy line?

### Asking for Permission

You know that when setting up your email newsletter mailing lists, you should always have a customer opt-out to keep you out of the dreaded spam filters. If you can get a double opt-in from your customers who want to receive your newsletters, than that is even better. (A double opt-in is where they sign up for the newsletter through a website leaving their email address, and then receive an email asking them to click on a link.) This not only helps you know that they typed in a good email address, but it also helps you to know that this person really wants to receive your fabulous library information.

This is one of the first steps to building that one-to-one relationship with customers. Your customers need to know that you won't spam them with nonlibrary information, that you won't sell their name to another vendor, and that they can trust you to do what you say you will do. It seems simple, but how many times have you gotten burned signing up to download a white paper only to be inundated by countless emails from other vendors? Building this relationship is all about listening to what your customers' wants and needs are—not just acting on what you think they want. Customer-centered marketing depends on your listening skills as well as research into what behaviors they display. This isn't easy. You need to look at every related statistic that you can get your hands on.

You'll find your first piece of customer information in your cardholder data. Through your system, you should be able to download some specific information about your customer that will help you build that relationship. Work through the privacy pieces with your cardholder database administrator. For example, they can leave off names, birthdates, and card and phone numbers while still giving you the rich demographic data you need, such as how many of your cardholders are under the age of 13, how many live in a certain zip code, or how many have checked out an item in the last month or year. All of this data along with the general demographic data about your community from the last census, such as what percentage speak a language other than English or how many make over $50,000 a year, can help you better assess where you start in building a relationship.

The second place to collect data is from your online portals. Make sure your web person has added Google Analytics to all your web pages so that you can track and graph which pages are visited most often. Gather stats from your blog views, from your Facebook and Twitter pages, and from anywhere else you can get them.

**MOXIE TIP** Ever heard of Seth Godin? He has some great information on his blog about the term he made popular in 2008, "permission marketing." *Permission* marketing explains how marketers can use permission from their customers to create content that people want and to engage them in a conversation about something that they care about first, for example: "Are you interested in mysteries? We are too, here is some information you will like." Consider this approach instead of the opposite way of beginning the conversation, with an *interruption* marketing tactic like "Sign up for our eNewsletter today!"

Another term for *permission marketing* is *inbound marketing*, which attracts people to your message. *Interruption marketing* is also called *outbound marketing*, where you push your message in front of people whether they are interested or not, like most forms of print and broadcast advertising. If you are tired of the *spray and pray* method and would like to know more, check out Seth's blog at http://sethgodin.typepad.com.

You can also gather information through the traditional ways of surveys, feedback forms, focus groups, telemarketing, word of mouth, and a lot of other places.

## eNEWSLETTERS

The next thing on your social media to-do list is an eNewsletter. eNewsletters aren't necessarily considered to be social, since they are more than likely a one-way push-out of information; but you can make them social by using links to connect your customers back to your website or blog for more information, or by adding a call to action with a link to sign up for an event or a poll or survey.

But first, you need people to send your eNews to. The trick to growing your email list is more than just putting up a link on your website saying "Sign up now!" People are inundated with email in their inbox, so you want to make sure that they know what you will give them and that it will be of benefit to them. Many online marketers let you download white papers or quilt patterns if you give them your email address. Libraries can also entice readers with freebies like "timely information to keep your child reading," or "exclusive invitations to library events."

Ask for email addresses at every opportunity—on paper survey forms, or on drawings for book giveaways or advanced author tickets. Your contacts should always be permission-based, and be sure to offer subscribers several to choose from, depending on how you would like to segment your subscribers. Be sure to let subscribers know that you respect their privacy and that their email address will be used only for library business. Always add that unsubscribing is easy and can be done at any time.

**Tips for Successful eNewsletters:**

MOXIE TIP

- Incorporate your logo and graphic standards into your eNewsletter.
- Don't use too many graphics or photos. Remember, more and more people will be looking at your email from their phone or other mobile devices, so you don't want to slow down the loading of content.
- Keep your writing short and to the point. You can send them to a web page for more on a particular topic if you need the room.
- When writing, ask yourself, "So what?" Make sure people have a reason to open your email and an engaging subject line to get them to look at it and not just delete the email.
- Only send out as many emails as you told your subscribers you would—e.g., once a week, or once a month.
- Ask your IT folks to set up an SPF record and a DKIM record on your DNS (Domain Name Service) provider to keep your emails out of the spam filters. As defined by Wikipedia, SPF (Sender Policy Framework) is a simple email validation system. The SPF type of record identifies which mail servers are permitted to send email on behalf of your domain. DKIM (Domain Keys Identified Mail) is a method used to validate the authenticity of incoming emails. Both of these records will help save you from being flagged for using a forged sender address.

**Tips for Staying Out of the Spam Box Include:**

MOXIE TIP

- Never use deceptive headers, from-names, reply-tos, or subject lines.
- An unsubscribe link must always be provided.
- Remove those who have unsubscribed from your list within 10 days.

- The unsubscribe link in your email must be working for at least 30 days after you send the email.
- You must include your physical mailing address on the email (it is usually in tiny print on the bottom).
- Avoid phrases like "FREE!" "Click here!" or USING ALL CAPS with lots of exclamation points!!!!! Also avoid coloring fonts with bright red or using only photos with no text explanation.
- Learn more about the CAN-SPAM Act of 2003, this federal act sets out the guidelines that need to be followed to be a reputable emailer. Go to the Federal Trade Commission's Business Center (http://www.ftc.gov/tips-advice/business-center) to read the entire act.
- Most commercial email providers have a spam filter criteria list that you can run your eNewsletter through before you send it, and it will give you a rating of how *spammy* your content is.
- Different systems use different algorithms for spam filtering, and they are always changing, so unfortunately there are no guarantees. You just want to make sure you don't get reported as a spammer; being polite by getting permission to send in the first place will go a long way.

## GETTING ORGANIZED

Social media is fun! It is addictive and easy to get sucked into the social vortex. To succeed in social media, be sure to plan first, keeping in mind what you will able to do within the confines of your time limitations. Before jumping in, define your goals, noting why you are adding certain media channels. Write down your top five social media goals and objectives, put them next to your computer, and stick to them! Also, be sure to add details about your social media campaigns to the "tactics" section on your content calendar.

Chances are that everyone is telling you to be on social media, and they all have their favorites; but how do you know what venues make the most sense for your time investment? Here is a short guide that will help you determine where you should be for your customers.

1. Facebook: Dominated by 35- to 54-year-olds, mostly white. Women are the most active. Visual content dominates. Used more as a personal network for friends and family as well as personal expression.
   - Libraries can harness Facebook for a variety of marketing and promotional opportunities. Use it to update your *friends* on programs and events, interesting author or book reviews from other sources, and especially to plug any blog posts or other social media posts you want people to be able to *like* and *share* easily. Pay attention to the insights or analytics page to see when people are checking their Facebook page, days and times, and the particular demographic whom you are seeing friending the library. Pay close attention and keep track of the posts you put up that have the greatest *likes* and *shares* and do more of that type to engage your customers more. Good visuals will always gain more likes, and the more likes and shares your post gets, the higher the ranking Facebook will give it, and the more Facebook will send it out to more of your *friends*. Keep status updates to no more than three per day.
2. Twitter: Dominated by 25- to 44-year-olds, mostly white. Evenly split between men and women. This works more as an information network with it being the go-to place for instant reactions to events. Considered microblogging.

- Libraries can use Twitter to re-tweet articles and posts of interest from other community organizations, as well as your own information. People who don't use Twitter see it as a microblog for lonely people talking about their cats, but it has become a go-to place for up-to-the-minute information that is being used by the news media, emergency groups, and other organizations. A great use for your Twitter feed is for library emergency closures due to floods or power outages. If you attach hashtags from other local feeds, such as your town or county and police services, you will have an immediate reach to more people than those who generally follow you.

3. Pinterest: Dominated by 35- to 44-year-old white/non-Hispanic, upper-income women. Visual content dominates, especially that related to lifestyle, design, and products.

   - Libraries can use Pinterest in a variety of ways. Set up boards with book reviews, infographics, or crafts to go along with children's stories. Some of our more popular boards are artwork and historic library photos from all over the world. You can also use Pinterest to promote your summer reading program, with additional activities people can do at home that go along with your theme. Do a search for other library Pinterest sites to pin from and to get additional ideas of what's hot.

4. YouTube: Dominated by 25- to 44-year-olds. The world's largest search engine behind Google. Displays only video content and works for all levels of engagement from DIY and TED Talks to those silly cats.

   - Libraries can use this visual marketing tool for training your customers how to download books from your website as well as adding video content to your YouTube channel that can then be integrated into your other social media channels by linking or embedding your video. Do video tours of your facilities, interview staff members or funders, conduct book talks, and tell your library story through video. Don't make them too long; 30 seconds to two minutes is plenty. If they run longer than that, break it up into several segments.

5. LinkedIn: Dominated by 35- to 54-year-old white men. Used for business networking and career enhancement.

   - LinkedIn company pages for your library are easy to accomplish, and when you do, you will be surprised how many of your employees are already on LinkedIn. Libraries can use their LinkedIn page to promote business databases, computer classes, and nonfiction author visits. Company pages need to be started and managed through a personal page; there is no separation between personal and professional, so as you add information to your company page, you are also reaping the rewards for your personal pages. Merging your personal and professional can be worrisome to some people, but because of the professional nature of the LinkedIn network, you shouldn't worry. Try to post at least once a week, with something you have read or a link to a great library story in a newspaper or other media outlet. From your personal page, sign into LinkedIn Groups, where you will learn how to make your job easier. A few of the current ones I use are: American Library Association, Innovative Marketing, Marketing Public Libraries, PR Professionals, Social Media Marketing, Once a Day Marketing, Social Media for Nonprofit Organizations, and Urban Libraries Council, as well as several local organizations.

6. Instagram: Dominated by 28- to 34-year-old black and Hispanic users. This channel is gaining in popularity with other demographics as well. Displays images and six-second videos, which can be used alone or added to other social media channels. The channel used

to be full of lots of food and selfies but is now expanding, especially with colleges and event coordinators, to publicize the latest events!

- Search your local Instagram channels to like, follow, and connect with Instagram users in your community. Use hashtags and @ mentions to spread the word. Be sure to look up a hashtag before you use it, in case it has been taken over by a group that you may not want to be associated with. Take your mascot out and ask people to take selfies with it and tag you on their Instagram feed. Post photos from a special event, during banned-books week and take photos of people reading a banned book. New York Public Library does a #bookfacefriday where people interact with books and upload their photos. A college library I've seen does an Instagram feed of students sleeping in the library to get the word across; if you sleep, you might have your photo taken.

7. Google+: Dominated by 18- to 34-year-old men. Free videoconferencing feature (Google Hangouts) is well used. Known as the place to talk about technology and all things geek, Google+ is gaining momentum because of some of the changes Facebook has made to the way they display updates. When you sign up for a Gmail account, you automatically get a Google+ account. The competition between Google+ and Facebook is escalating.

- Libraries can use Google+ in a similar way as Facebook with the addition of more tech information.

---

**MOXIE TIP**

**The *T-shirt* Explanation of Social Media Channels:**

Facebook: I like drinking beer
Twitter: I'm drinking #beer
YouTube: Watch me drink a beer
Instagram: Beautiful beer photos
Pinterest: How I make my beer
LinkedIn: Skills—Beer making

---

There are literally billions of bytes of information out there on social media, telling you what it is, where you should be, which ones are best for what purpose. This can be very overwhelming, and the information changes practically daily! Having realistic expectations about your social media is important. Remember that the greatest use of these tools is for making personal connections with your customers and supporters. Many libraries are disappointed when they put up a Facebook page and don't gain 1,000 friends the first week. You need to make sure all of your social channels are integrated in a way that they feed off of each other; that way, you are catching your customers where they already are and not trying to get them to be a Google+ user if everyone they know uses Facebook. That is why keeping track of your page metrics so you can see the steady growth of your pages is important. Don't be fooled by the social media gurus who can guarantee that your YouTube video will go viral if you just do X, Y, and Z. Having patience and diversification, just like investing in the stock market, will lead to growth in numbers and popularity for your social media channels.

Because the algorithms for social media change so fast, and because the networks are constantly updating and tweaking their sites, any information on how to sign up or work with settings in social channels that was published more than six months ago is suspect. Some of the easiest and best ways to get a handle on social media channels are through info-graphics—check out Visually (http://www.visual.ly) for some of the best. The social media sites themselves are also increasingly putting up hints and tips on how to use their sites; they of course have a vested interest in making their sites easy to use.

Your social media profile is the next piece you need to pay attention to. For each social channel, you will be asked to add a profile picture or avatar. This is a version of your logo that has been designed to be seen as a square or circle (in the case of Google+ and You-Tube). This avatar is the face of your library, and it is important that it be designed as such and isn't your current logo squished into a box shape. Take the time and have it done correctly as part of your branding efforts.

Next, you will be asked to add in your name, location, website URL, and links to other social media accounts. Some have additional fields where they ask for a short bio, contact information, and hours of operation. Sites such as Twitter and Facebook also let you add custom background images as well as banner photos. Take full advantage of these customizable features to help with your library branding. When people are searching for your library, this is the first information that they see, and they will make decisions on your credibility as they look at it. All of your channels need to have the same branded qualities; keep them interesting by changing out the photos and banner, but keep your avatar and backgrounds the same so that people will know they have found the right library at a glance.

**MOXIE TIP** No matter what social media channels you decide to dive into, make sure that you go through the process to claim your name or vanity URL on all of them that you can think of. Once your name has been taken, it is impossible to get it back, and someone else may start posting as you. You can add your desired username into NameChk (http://www.namechk.com) and it will show you which social media channels are available with that name. Your URL should be consistent across all channels and consistent with your website so that people can find you.

## BLOGS AND VLOGS

Blogging is the new staple of the modern communications manager. Along with email and your website, your blog is at the center of your marketing strategy.

Using your blog as the hub of your social media strategy not only gives you fresh content to work from on a regular basis, but it also can help to broaden your reach in the community. The library blog is one place where you can accept postings from all library staff as well as any community member. The great thing about libraries is that no matter what someone writes about, you can relate it back somehow to your mission or services. Through a blog, your library can tell its story, discuss newsworthy events, and share resources quickly with members. Your blog can also be shared through a network of your local blogging community, by asking them to do guest blogs for you or by asking them to cite resources from the library in their posts.

Blogs also improve search engine results to your library. Google uses spiders to look for keywords in page titles, so every new post you publish to the web will help increase your website's chances of being found. Use your blog to add members to your eNewsletter mailing lists. If your blog is organized thematically, or by different types of entries, it can also help with adding customers to specific segmented newsletters. For example, a blog post about local history might ask people to sign up for an email newsletter called "Then and Now," which is full of information about the library's history archives or photo collection.

Send people from your blog to your other social media channels. Ask them to share information about a poetry contest you are having, using the share buttons in the blog—this makes it easy to distribute further.

If you are concerned about people abusing the blog or posting inappropriate remarks, consider setting up moderated comments so you can okay them before they are added to the blog posting. Blogging platforms have a notification service that you can set up when you start your blog pages. The service will send you an email when a comment is made, and then you can go in and approve or disapprove the comment.

Blogging platforms let you embed various types of widgets into your blog to help your readers share your content. They can also subscribe to your newsletter and find you on other social media channels. Using an RSS (Real Simple Syndication) feed from your blog to your webpage, you can automatically add your new blog headline to a box on your home page to gain attention. Have your web developer add in the coding for you. Adding an RSS link to your blog will also encourage people who use a RSS feed aggregator to link to it, so they will get automatic updates every time you publish. For a list of aggregators, go to RSS Reader (http://www.rss-readers.org).

When choosing a blogging platform, find out what sorts of statistics and data reports it can provide for you. Most include the top four metrics, which are:

1. Visits: This metric will measure the number of visits to your blog, either by total numbers or unique visitors, or both.
2. Traffic: This metric shows you where your visitors are coming from. Did they just come in from a Google search, or did they come in from a referral such as your Facebook post about the new blog post?
3. Pages Per Visit: Basically, this is visitor retention. If your readers look at two or more pages per visit, you are doing well.
4. Bounce: This important metric basically tells you how long they stayed on the page before they *bounced* off. Unlike a bounce from an email where you probably have a bad address, the bounce rate for your blog is important to track because it lets you know if your readers are finding something of interest. Sometimes shown as a percentage, you want to have it stay below 65 percent. These metrics can also be seen as number of pages visited or number of seconds visited. This would logically show that the higher the number of pages visited or the longer they are reading your site, the more engaged your readers are. Another link to look at is how many visitors referred to your blog from your social media posts and what their bounce rate is. It would follow that these are your most engaged readers, and you want their numbers to go up!

These analytics will enhance your other data-gathering efforts and will help you make sure that your social media marketing strategies are on the right track.

There are numerous blogging platforms such as WordPress (http://www.wordpress.org and http://www.wordpress.com) and Typepad (http://www.typepad.com) are the most popular for libraries and nonprofits. Others to check out include Squarespace (http://www.squarespace.com), Tumblr (http://www.tumblr.com), and Blogger (http://www.blogger.com). Look for one with publishing tools that are simple and usable, with the emphasis on readable content and not fancy themes or backgrounds. Remember, more and more of your customers will be looking at your blog post on your phone and just want fast and readable access to information. Each platform varies with the level of customization it accommodates, and whether it can be embedded directly into your website. Ease of use is one of the most important features to look for; you do not want to have to do HTML coding or have the site be so hard to use that it discourages you from wanting to use it.

Tumblr is making its mark as a blogging platform that has more of a visual theme, sort of a social network built around a blog. If you are planning for a lot of your content to consist of photographs and videos, you may want to see if Tumblr would work better for your needs. For one of the most customizable platforms, WordPress will have what you need through their many third-party plug-ins. WordPress.com is the free version that stays on the WordPress server; hence your blog will have a domain name ending in WordPress.com. WordPress.org is a full-featured customizable suite, mostly free with some features at a minimal cost. Look through both versions to see which one will fit your needs. Typepad is also hosted on their own server and has a monthly price structure depending on what features you are using.

Before setting up your blog, do your homework. YouTube (http://www.youtube.com) has some great videos on starting a blog with step-by-step instructions. Search for the specific blogging platform you are using (WordPress, Blogger, etc.) and pick the most recent one so that the instructions given match what you are looking at on your computer. Many of the blogging websites have very good step-by-step videos also, but you may have to sign up in order to access them. Go to Meetup (http://www.meetup.com) and do a search for *blog* or *blogger* along with what town you live in; search results will bring back local bloggers in your area as well as people interested in blogging. If there isn't already a Meetup group set up for bloggers, you can start one in the library! Learning together in a group setting is always a great way to get your questions answered and to help your library message get out to group members.

Having a blog increases your webpage's search engine optimization (SEO). Spiders (sometimes called webcrawlers) that scour the web looking for prioritized keywords find and index your blog content headlines, categories, and content; this helps people searching the Internet find your information faster. If you are blogging about a current event, check out the trending keywords in the current social media channels and make sure one of those keywords is used in your headline to raise your SEO. For example, you can look up trending hashtags in your area on Twitter, and if #stormchaser is being highly used, then you can title your library blog headline "Looking for Calm in the Storm?" then use #stormchaser in your keywords to help bring your blog post higher on online search results.

When one of your library staff members sends you an unasked-for blog post, thank them! These can be some of the best posts you'll get. Staff members generally have a multitude of passions and interests, and the blog gives them an outlet for expression. Don't make it mandatory that staff use their full name or a photo of themselves, but do ask for 500 words or less or about three good paragraphs. Blog posts that feature lists are some of the most shared. People love the five ways to help your child be a better reader, or the 10 most banned books. All those English majors that you work with might tend to think of this as a formal essay. Remind them they are writing for the masses, and to be personal and sincere, as well as to end the post with a call to action.

As with any marketing content, adding a call to action to your post makes it more powerful. You may ask readers to sign up for the new eNewsletter, send a poem into the poetry contest, sign up for the summer reading program, like your Facebook page, donate to your crowd funding campaign, or countless other things. By getting a response, you are not only engaging your readers, but gathering valuable information and learning more about them.

A *vlog* is basically a more visual blogging system, which uses video. Most blogging platforms provide you with a way to embed videos, which can be especially useful if you are doing an interview with an author or showing how to download a book onto your iPad. You can also have fun with a vlog, telling a great library story by asking a four-year-old about her favorite part of summer reading.

Here are some blog/vlog content ideas:

- History, behind the scenes, or about us information. Interview the staff member who orders books and materials for the library. How do they decide what to buy, and what it takes to get a book processed and put on the shelf? Strap a digital camera on a book, turn it on, and run it through your automated materials handler.

- Events: Interview customers about their favorite book made into a movie to highlight an upcoming movie series. Video kids playing Minecraft at a library event and then interview them about their favorite video games.

- Volunteers: Interview the volunteer who stacks and tags all the books before the sale about what it takes to put on a book sale with thousands of books. Or video the library mascot high-fiving kids in your downtown. Then have the volunteer talk about why they love being a library mascot.

- Current events in your community: Interview a customer to find out what their favorite fall activities are around town—favorite corn maze, pumpkin patch, haunted house, etc.

- A pertinent story that relates to your mission and goals: Interview and video a child reading at the beginning of the summer and then again at the end to highlight their advancing reading skills.

- In-person interviews with a local celebrity or an expert: Tap into a local college and ask an art professor who their greatest influence was. Highlight the artist's work with photos.

- Highlight donors or fundraising activities: Talk to a community donor and ask why they decided to put a donation of money to the library in their will.

- Ideas that play off www.TodayinHistory.com, or Chase's Event Calendar. Or found on presentation/document sharing sites like SlideShare (http://www.slideshare.com), Prezi (http://www.prezi.com), or Haiku Deck (http://www.haikudeck.com).

- Set up a personal page on the news aggregator Alltop (http://www.alltop.com). Then you can select and view trending topics to get post ideas from. I love the posts under the "Lifehacker" heading that tell you useful information on do-it-yourself ideas with materials you can find around the house.

- Don't forget about the visuals! Look for copyright free photos and graphics to add to your blog or vlog by using Creative Commons (http://www.creativecommons.org).

A one-on-one relationship is the next wave in marketing. Libraries walk a fine line as they gather information to better market to their patrons but need to keep their personal information protected. Asking customers to opt in to newsletters is the first step to creating a relationship where you are giving them what they want, not what you think they need. Using library card data and online portals is the beginning of permission marketing. Don't force messages on your patrons; attract them to your message by giving them information they actually want to hear. Social media is the new way to create one-on-one relationships. Make sure you have goals laid out for what you would like to accomplish before you begin. This will help you narrow what social media outlets to use and what content to post. Blogging is a necessity for the modern communications manager. Blogs or vlogs not only let you communicate about the goings on at the library, but can be a forum to allow community members and staff to create exciting and interesting content. Do a little research to find out which blogging platform will give you the metrics you need. Finally, eNewsletters are a way to give more in-depth information about the library. Make them easy to read, make sure they load quickly, and above all, make sure you are answering the question "So what?"

## REFERENCE

Rosen, N. (2012). *Chatter Marketing.* Austin, TX: Emerald Book Company.

# 6

# SOCIAL MEDIA BEST PRACTICES

Social media is an ephemeral marketing scheme—always in flux and changing. As soon as you get your posting flow down, you can bet the channels will change, and you will have to relearn them again. The best place to find *how-to* information about using social media is on the social media sites themselves, or you can go to YouTube (http://www.youtube .com) to find video instructions. Just beware of any videos that are over six months old. Because this is an ever-changing landscape, this chapter describes the best practices of these media channels instead of offering step-by-step guides to set up your profiles.

To try to straighten out how you refer to your online contacts through social media sites, here is a short reference:

- Facebook: People become *friends* with each other and *fans* of an organization's page; they like, comment, and share.
- Twitter: People become *followers* of other users; they favorite, reply, and retweet.
- YouTube: People become a *subscriber* or *friend* of other users; they view, like, and comment.
- Pinterest: People are *followers* of others; they like, comment, and repin.
- Instagram: People are *followers*; they like and comment.
- LinkedIn: People are *followers*; they like, comment, and share.
- Blogs/Vlogs: People become a *subscriber* of the blog when they sign up to use their RSS feed or have updates sent to them through their news feed aggregator.

When adding content to these sites, you are updating your status, tweeting, streaming, and posting. That is a lot to keep track of!

**MOXIE TIP** When starting down the social media highway, use the 80/20 rule: 80 percent of the content you share should be third-party content or connecting with third parties. The 20 percent should be about your organization. Thinking in this way will ensure that your library is seen as a community organizer, and not too *spammy* and showing it's all about me!

## SOCIAL MEDIA POLICIES

Many organizations who have numerous social media sites have taken the time to put together a social media policy. This policy covers how the information on the site will be posted as well as if sites will be monitored, or moderated by staff. Decide ahead of time who from the public you will allow to post on any of your social media sites. Have your external social media policy and disclaimer in place, and add it to the other policies section on your website, so you can refer people to it.

External social media policies should cover:

- A statement linking the mission of the library to your participation with social networking channels. You may include the idea that social media is considered an additional online resource that the library provides.

- A definition of social media channels, such as, "an application which allows users to share information." It can include but is not limited to the library blog, Twitter, Facebook, and YouTube.

- A disclaimer about use by minors. You probably have this in your other policies, but it can be reinstated again as it pertains to social media. An example would be: "as the Library does not act in place of or in the absence of a parent and is not responsible for enforcing any restrictions which a parent or guardian may place on a minor's use of this resource."

- A statement about privacy and collection of personal information, which you also probably have in other policies, and how it pertains to social media. For example: "the Library does not collect, maintain, or otherwise use personal information stored on any third-party site in any way other than to communicate with users of the social media site. By permission given by the user for contact outside the site, the Library may use their contact information for means of recruitment of volunteers or for reference help. Users should be aware that third-party websites have their own privacy policies and should use their privacy settings appropriately."

- A statement referring to moderated comments and posts on social networking sites, that the library respects different opinions and will monitor and review comments for relevancy and content. You may want to spell out what types of comments or visuals (video or photos) will be removed, such as obscene or racist content, organized political activity, plagiarized material, personal attacks or insults, personal information published without consent, hyperlinks not directly related to the discussion, and commercial spam.

- The library is granted the rights to reproduce comments or posts for use in other promotional materials such as quotes in the newsletter or annual report. Posts may be edited for space as long as they retain the intent of the original.

- A disclaimer statement, which relieves the library from liability regarding any interaction that takes place, that it does not endorse or review any content on outside networking sites or that sites may be reviewed periodically by library staff and may be terminated without notice to subscribers.

The above ideas are pulled from content from Social Media Policies from Newton Free Library (Massachusetts), Berkeley Public Library (California), and Whitman Public Library (Massachusetts).

Having others post on your social media channels is what being social is all about! At the time of this writing, Facebook has a posting moderation function that you can set up whereby posts from others are held until you allow them to post. Your blog as well as many of the other channels have similar settings. Many organizations are wary to let people comment on their different social media channels. What if they say something bad? The moderation helps you prevent inappropriate postings. Just remember, you want comments! You want to know what your customers like and don't like. Don't think of negative comments as being bad; think of them as opportunities. The first step you need to take is to try to figure out exactly what the negative comment is based on. What was the goal of the person making the comment? Was it a problem with something that is easily seen and responded to, such as a member who returned a book but was still charged an overdue fee? Or was it a general criticism of the customer not agreeing with a certain policy, or were they just wanting to vent about the rude treatment they received? Many people use social media to criticize, but also to suggest solutions such as "Please lower your shelves of large print books; I am in a wheelchair and can't reach half of the collection." Or sometimes it is just an outright attack, such as "I hate your library, every time I come in I can never find what I want." This sort of comment is much harder to address since they don't give you anything specific to go by. It is hard to tell if they really are looking for a response or they are just being a *troll*, in that they are just trying to get some sort of response for their attack. Statements such as "Libraries are wasting my tax money! Who needs them now that we have the Internet?" fall into this sort of comment.

Working with customer feedback on all levels is the mission of the library staff. People who work in libraries are inherently problem-solvers and want to help our customers resolve theirs. But with social media comments, rather than getting into a tit-for-tat conversation through the comment section, it is a good idea to have some basic guidelines or procedures for handling negative comments, as rare as they truly are. Because you are monitoring all of your channels, you should be able to respond quickly to comments, both positive and negative. Responding quickly to a complaint is key; it lets the customer know that a real person is on the other side of the computer screen and that the library is interested in making customer service their top priority. Jump in and say something, even if you don't have all the facts yet, with a response like "Thank you for your comment, we are aware of the situation and we don't know the cause, but we will get back to you as soon as we do." Many people who make negative comments just want to know that someone has listened to them. Remember, social media is about relationship building, and you want to show empathy and a human voice and not come off as a robot. Accept responsibility and apologize for the problem if it is truly the library's fault. Don't make excuses or shift blame; by doing so, you may inadvertently escalate the situation.

If you cannot get to the background of the negative comment, ask the person to call or email you directly so that you can get the matter solved. Because many people are more interested in being heard that actually resolving the problem, chances are you will get few who actually contact you. Remember, others are watching your response, not just the person who commented. If the situation is taken offline to resolve, remember to post the resolution so that others watching will know that the library took care of it. It may be a change in procedures or a resolution in another way, but you want to show that your library is interested in being transparent and solving customer problems.

You can always find a silver lining in a criticism, unless you have those snarky trolls trying to stir something up; in that case, you will probably find it is better to say "Thank you for your comment" and not respond any further, especially if it looks like the troll is trying to get you into a never-ending debate on something. Don't delete their comments, just ignore them; most people who are savvy with social media can see through a troll's comments and won't think badly about your not responding. Unless it is a case in which the person is using racist language or inappropriate swear words, etc., those comments should be taken down, and that person should be blocked from commenting. A few negative comments with sincere responses of addressing the problem can go a long way in showing that the library is social media–savvy as well as customer-friendly, thus adding to your credibility as being part of the online community.

## Internal Social Media Policy or Guidelines

If you are fortunate enough to have others helping you with social media updates, or if you just want to show your board what policies you are following, you will want to have written guidelines to refer to. Some libraries add employee posting information to their general social media policies, while others do a separate policy or guidelines statement. An example of guidelines should include:

- Be transparent and state that you work for the library.
- Never represent the library in a false or misleading way.
- Post meaningful and respectful on-topic comments.
- Use common sense and common courtesy.
- When disagreeing with other's opinions, be polite and appropriately address the disagreement. If you find the situation becoming antagonistic, ask the communications manager for advice or disengage from the dialogue in a polite manner that reflects well on the library.
- Be smart about protecting yourself, your privacy, and the library's confidential information.

**MOXIE TIP** Every social media manager can use Google Alerts (http://www .google.com/alerts) to keep track of what the world is saying about you. This free service will send you an email when a keyword that you have set up is mentioned. You should set up a Google Alert for each of the following, as well as any others that would directly pertain to your library:

- The library's full name as well as any variations on the name that are commonly used
- The library director's name and names of your board members or Friends of the Library president

- Your library's tagline or other special promotional words you use
- You may want to add in your city and county names along with the word *library* to catch outside references

## FACEBOOK

Facebook can be defined as an online social networking application that allows users to create a profile, upload photos and videos, post updates, and make comments on shared posts in order to keep in touch with members of their personalized network, known as their *friends*. Interactions are published in a news feed that can be accessed through the Internet or through a smartphone app.

When setting up your Facebook page, be sure to look at the "email notifications" section and check the "send notifications to [your email]," so that you receive emails when people post or comment on your page. I use the Pages Manager app (go to your smartphone's app store to get it) on my phone instead, so that the notifications aren't mixed into the hundreds of emails I get. I want to be able to respond quickly to comments. There are also other media management tools that you can use such as MediaFeedia (http://www.mediafeedia .com), which will also send you real-time updates.

Add a "like" button to your blog or website by going to the Social Plugins page on Facebook at https://developers.facebook.com/docs/plugins and click the "Like Button" link. Customize the widget and press the "Get Code" button, then insert the code into your blog template or website. When people click on this "like" button, it shows up on their Facebook news feed, which shows their friends that they support your library.

Search the Facebook Help Center at http://www.facebook.com/help for specifics on setting up security and managing your page. Make sure you have at least two people as administrators to the page in case one leaves or something urgent needs to be posted.

Use your Facebook Insights (not seen in personal Facebook accounts), found under your administrator settings, to view your built-in page analytics. With these Insights, you can see demographic data breakdowns as well as which of your posts are the most read, shared, and liked, and add more of those types. If you are using Facebook to promote a contest, be sure to look at their guidelines, under http://www.facebook.com/page_guidelines.php, as far as what is acceptable, or you may find your feed has been blocked or content taken down. See the Suggested Readings section of this book for the link to a great infographic on this subject.

**MOXIE TIP**    Keeping Facebook exposure in mind, a good trick is to have at least 10 or more people that you can count on (they may be staff) to like and share every Facebook post you put up. This will help boost your engagement numbers in your analytics slightly, and it will also boost the amount of people who see the post.

Look for trending hashtags (used in Facebook, Twitter, Instagram, and other social channels) that are used in your community, and make a list of them to help expand the reach of your posts, especially if there are certain topics that the library can show some expertise on. Don't add too many hashtags, three is plenty; and don't add in ones that will not do you any good, like #awesome. That just makes you look dumb.

Decide whether you want your Facebook posts to automatically share with other social media channels, such as Instagram or Twitter, and vice versa. To do that you will need to go into the profile settings of the other channels and log in with your Facebook credentials. There are various debates on the value of automating and linking your channels. I would suggest not doing it because each channel carries your message in a slightly different way. You also want your content to be authentic and relevant to the demographic that channel is reaching. If your Instagram feed is predominantly teen boys, they don't care about the new storytime you posted on Facebook for your thirtysomething moms.

**Tips for Facebook:**

*MOXIE TIP*

- Use engaging photos with text overlaid called *memes*. Memes get shared at a higher percentage than just a photo and can be used on multiple channels. Use PicMonkey (http://www.picmonkey.com) to design memes if you don't have a graphics person on staff.
- Keep your Facebook posts Like-able; there is no Dislike option.
- Keep your post no longer than 140 characters, so you can also use them for other social media channels.
- Explore the use of the Facebook Events system to invite your fans to share and RSVP to a special library event, or to leave comments on the event wall about what they would like to see at the event.
- Shorten links by copying your long URL link and pasting it into a URL-shortening application such as Bitly (https://www.bitly.com). Then take the shortened link a paste it back into your post. If you sign up for a Bitly account, it also shows you the tracking for how many times the link is clicked on.

## Facebook Ads

The changes in the Facebook algorithm interface during 2014 have sent many businesses to try out Facebook ads so all of their followers can see their posts. Facebook has been experimenting with the *who-sees-what* information for some time and is likely to keep changing those terms. The constantly changing interface can make it very frustrating to take the time to build your follower base to 5,000 people and then look at your stats to see that only 100 viewed it. The algorithm takes into account many different things, like how many likes and shares the post had, if the content was fresh or generated from somewhere else, keywords that may be trending, and more. Some libraries are trying to work around this by buying Facebook advertising. To do this, you can go to http://www.facebook.com/advertising.

If you decide to bite the bullet and pay for Facebook advertising, for example for a special event or fundraising activity, keep the following in mind:

- What is your goal, can it be measured, and how? Pick a specific goal that you are trying to achieve, such as a 10 percent increase in people signing up for your eNewsletter off of your website. This is called a website conversion as an objective. This goal is specific enough that you can tell if you met it with the ad.
- When you create your ad, you will be asked what the advertising objective is. In other words what do you want people to do when they see your ad? You may want people to sign up for an event or visit your website to see a special feature about a new library service you

are offering. Ads are shown in the right-hand column of Facebook or in the Newsfeed on mobile devices.

- There are no set prices for Facebook ads. When you create the ad, you will have budget and bidding options to choose from. You can set a daily amount for what you want to spend, so that after that amount is spent, the ad will go away. You can also choose a lifetime budget, which is the amount you want to spend over the lifetime of the ad campaign by setting your own start and stop dates. If you choose this option, you will also need to set your CPM (cost per impression) or CPC (cost per click). An interesting feature of Facebook advertising is that you pay only for the impressions or clicks that your ad receives. Using a clickable ad to a specific page on your website to sign up for the monthly eNewsletter is a great way to test how the ad works. A well-targeted ad to one area of your segmented audiences, especially if it is in your prime Facebook demographic, can be very effective.

- Make sure your ad is well designed and well written. The ad must have a photo, and the best size to upload would be 1,200 x 627 pixels. The photo cannot contain more than 20 percent text, and if it is clickable, be sure it takes viewers to a specific page that has a call to action so that you can measure results. To see a summary of how your ad is doing, check the metrics on the Ads Manager page.

- Social media advertising is a dynamic and fluid tool. It is important for you to keep an eye on social media, to know what works best for your needs.

- For more information on Facebook ads, go to http://www.facebook.com/ads/create. Facebook has pages and pages of information to help step you through the entire process.

## TWITTER

Twitter can be defined as a microblogging social networking service. This free service allows members to send their *tweets* by a smartphone app or through an online computer. Anyone can follow public Twitter accounts, which are sometimes linked to special conversations or themes using a # (hashtag). You can use certain keyword hashtags to do searches for conversations. It is considered microblogging because you are limited to 140 characters for your tweet, which also includes any hyperlinks and your Twitter name or *handle*.

Best practices with Twitter include the general list of tips (e.g., make your posts engaging; use photos, videos, and hashtags), as well as using a more direct approach with tweet conversations. Twitter can raise awareness faster than other social media channels, so many people refer to it on a daily basis as often as they would a messaging application. Twitter followers are enticed to tweet while watching television, playing video games, and watching sporting events and concerts, but there are also some useful applications for your library.

The accessibility and instantaneous feeds can be extremely helpful during crisis management (for example, during flood and fire evacuations), as well as helping bring awareness of the library to community events, such as live tweeting during concerts. A more advanced type of social media strategy that is being used with Twitter and other channels is called *real-time* marketing. This has been defined as personal content delivered across channels and connecting with customers in a meaningful way in the right place and time with relevant content. A great example of real-time marketing is when the Red Cross discussed disaster preparedness live on Twitter at the same time that the made-for-TV movie *Sharknado* was airing (Walter 2014). Using the trending hashtags #Sharknado and #RedCross, they added into the feed a conversation about what you should do in case of a natural disaster. Basically, this is like doing a library reference interview, with the marketer responding to an online conversation not as an interruption, but as a welcome addition. These conversations should have a consistent marketing strategy behind them, so you don't lose track in the moment. Tying your marketing to a current event takes some practice, and it may fall flat; but if you stay true to your messaging and branding, being involved with the conversation will help you look relatable to the community.

---

**MOXIE TIP**

**Tips for Twitter:**

- Connect with other tweeters in your area by going to http://www.twitter.com/search-advanced and doing an area or word search to find local *twits*.
- There is also a Twitter Nonprofits feed account where you can do a search for other local or national nonprofits. This will guide you to some of the ways other nonprofit marketers are using the channel.
- Learn to write brief posts. If you have a long post that you want to tweet, break it up into smaller posts instead of just adding a link to your Facebook page. The reason people like Twitter is that they can get a lot of information in a short amount of time. They really don't want to be clicking on links to read long posts.
- If you do need to put in a link for your blog post or webpage into your Twitter update, make sure the information in the first 30 characters has an impact to make people want to read on. Keeping your posts shorter than the 140 characters (including hashtags and your Twitter handle) will make them easier to retweet and will keep your name visible.
- Make your tweets interesting by mixing in a quote from someone famous, especially if they are humorous.
- Start "Ask a Question Monday," where you share interesting stories from library staff about the interesting questions they get asked. Of course, you want to leave out any obvious references to people, but these stories can make for some fun comments and gain some new questions from people reading your tweets.
- Follow Friday is an unofficial day where you ask your followers to follow others. Use the hashtag #ff to see who others are recommending you follow. Give positive mentions to other organizations in your community, and they will give them back to you.

---

Twitter, like other social media channels, is all about building relationships. Build relationships with others that you follow, admire, or relate to. Tweet public messages using @Whatever their Twitter name is to connect with them or comment on their latest contribution. Just remember that tweets are public, so don't just tweet "Right on @YourLibrariesHandle"; be more specific—for example, "The great staff @YourLibrariesHandle helped me land a new job. Thanks!" When you start talking about others, they will reciprocate, and that's where the social comes in. Don't just talk about what you are doing all the time; remember, marketing is about them, not you.

If you have multiple Twitter accounts to manage, you should use a social media management application such as TweetDeck (http://www.tweetdeck.com) or Hootsuite (http://www.hootsuite.com) to manage them. TweetDeck is owned by Twitter and helps you schedule and manage multiple Twitter feeds. The Hootsuite management application lets you share and schedule posts from your Twitter, Facebook, and LinkedIn accounts, all from one dashboard. Even if your organization isn't interested in having multiple Twitter accounts, using a management app to schedule, monitor mentions, and track the posts, or to keep track of the posts of just you or multiple people posting, is a great way to go. If your teen librarian wants a Twitter feed, and your children's staff also wants a feed, gather each of these feeds under a curated Twitter list group on your main library Twitter page; that way, you can cross promote to other followers and keep track of what is going out.

Increasing your media reach though Twitter is easy to do. Add your Twitter feed to your website or blog by embedding the profile widget. Your blog template may already have one incorporated on its site, or ask your web developer to find a widget and the coding to add a Twitter feed to your to the webpage through http://www.twitterforweb.com. If you are having great conversations on your feed, you want to be able to share that with people who are not using Twitter.

## YOUTUBE

YouTube is a social media service that allows users to share video content. This free service can be accessed through the Internet or by a smartphone app. YouTube, which is owned by Google, started out being used by ordinary people interested in sharing their videos and amateur films, but it is now used by companies, organizations, professional speakers, and more to show how-to videos, music and sports videos, and video content on every topic imaginable! Who would have predicted 20 years ago or more that you would be able to go to a video channel to look for information on any topic under the sun?

I recently rented a rug shampooer and took it apart to clean before I used it, which led to my having several leftover pieces when I put it back together! What did I do? I did a YouTube search for the model I was using, and a friendly guy popped up to show me exactly how to put the shampooer back together. The brilliance of the video wasn't that it was slick or pretty. In fact, the audio was sketchy and the lighting was bad. But it certainly gave me the information I needed and saved the day.

If you have something to talk about, video can be the perfect way to go. If you are not ready to start producing your own videos, set up your library YouTube channel by curating videos by others using the Playlist feature (https://www.youtube.com/yt/playbook/playlists .html). You can set up playlists with different sets of videos, one with videos from other libraries, celebrities reading books, or storytimes by those great Reading Rainbow folks. These lists will get your name out as well as get you into the YouTube search results. Direct your viewers directly to these by publishing the link in your other social media channels.

If you decide you are ready to produce your own videos, don't forget to upload your avatar and a banner (2,560 × 1,440 pixels) and fill in all of the information and links in your profile. Keep your videos short, around 30 seconds to a minute. Check out some of the built-in features that YouTube has, like royalty-free music and simple editing software that you can use. Use video tags and titles that maximize your SEO by adding the name of your library into the title. You can make screenshots of your videos to insert into your eNewsletters and link to them from your website and blog.

As of the time of this writing, here are a few successful (in my opinion) library-focused YouTube videos to get your creative juices flowing:

- The Dewey Decimal Rap (http://www.youtube.com/watch?v=NHiUQb5xg7A)
- Inside the Bodleian: Building a 21st Century Library (http://www.youtube.com/watch?v=v8r96cZC2lY)
- Amazing Flashmob (Library Singing) (http://www.youtube.com/watch?v=dsPDY606Joo)

YouTube currently has a nonprofit program, YouTube for Nonprofits, which you can apply for through Google after you set up your YouTube channel. This program gives you additional features through the application as well as step-by-step guides to fundraising campaigns, using the audio library, and more. The nonprofit channel also highlights some of the best nonprofit videos submitted to give you a lot of great ideas.

## INSTAGRAM

It is interesting how fast our cell phones became our cameras! Instagram is a photo- and video-sharing social network where you can share your activities through pictures with a short caption. Captured through an app on your smartphone or tablet, these photos are added to your Instagram feed but can also be automatically sent to other social media sites such as Facebook and Twitter. One of the popular features of Instagram is that it lets you apply a digital filter to your image to change the look of the photo, and continues to improve on their editing features. Instagram also uses a hashtag feature to let people search for certain themes or keywords, and short descriptions added to your posts will let people search for you. You can also take screenshots from your most successful photos on Facebook and Pinterest and upload them to Instagram. You can use Instagram to add 15-second videos that automatically play in Facebook. You can use this feature to show kids reading to dogs, your mascots on a parade float, the new self-checkout system, or a local poet reading their work for poetry month.

**Tips for Gaining Instagram Followers:**

MOXIE TIP

- Use popular hashtags—do a Google search to discover trending library or community hashtags. Some current ones are: #tbt (Throwback Thursday), #instadaily, and #photooftheday.
- Don't use more than three hashtags per post.
- Ask questions in the photo's caption box to drive people to comment.
- Use a tool like Iconosquare (http://www.iconosquare.com) to run a contest challenge on Instagram (for a fee).
- Use video in your feed.
- Ask Instagram celebrities to mention your account.
- Make sure your Instagram bio is filled out with branded hashtags, web links, and calls to action. Many people will look at the bio before they decide to follow you.
- Look under your profile options (the little gear symbol) to find People to Follow suggestions. If you follow them, chances are they will follow you.

Use your Instagram still photos to create a slideshow using Flipagram (http://www .flipagram.com). Instagram feeds can be seen on a PC but can only be used or added to through a phone or tablet Instagram app, so write a new smartphone with extra memory into next year's budget. Follow other libraries and see what they are posting. Some of the academic college libraries are doing great work, since they know that is where their customers are getting their information from; an interesting montage was done by the University of Maryland Library and can be found at https://storify.com/UMDLibraries/ libraries-on-instagram.

Some ideas for photos are:

- Books—photos of your new releases, interesting art made from books, or people doing interesting things with books like the #BookFaceFriday campaign
- Events—give people a hashtag to use as they share about Instagram photos from one of your events
- History—share copyright-free historical photos of your town from your archives, ask people to add in their own historical family photos
- Remodeling or construction—share construction behind the scenes updates via your Instagram feed to excite your community about the upcoming grand opening
- Behind the scenes—a sneak peek of a new exhibit, or piles of new books after a holiday closure, or lines of book carts with new books ready to go on the shelves
- Staff introductions—whether you have a librarian with a great bookish tattoo or one who raises fancy goldfish, you can introduce your staff's interests through photos
- Print goes digital—share your print material digitally by simply taking a photo of it and posting
- Use Instagram for a photo contest by using a certain hashtag or by adding their photos to a blog form link on your blog

## PINTEREST

Pinterest is a visual website used to share items that you have *pinned* and curated from online sources. These Pinterest boards are like a virtual bulletin board that you would have at home where you organize and pin interesting photos, visual book reviews, and other topics of interest that you would like to save and refer back to. Users can search and follow these subject area boards made by others as well as share their own boards with people who are interested in similar themes. One of the features of Pinterest is that when you click on a photo, it takes you back to the original source that it was pinned from. So clicking on a cocktail dress will take you back to the site where you can buy it. Pinterest is defined by the Urban Dictionary as 99 percent "pure virtual estrogen."

If you began your library Pinterest account before November 2012, be sure to go in and change the profile to be a business account. If you are just starting one, sign up as a business. Verify your website and select "Institution/Non-profit," as this will give you better access to statistics for your boards and page. Create at least five boards, adding maps and descriptions for each board to optimize your SEO, since Google picks up the keywords in the descriptions.

Pin content that is visually appealing—after all, that is what Pinterest is all about. Look up the *Little Free Library* that shows the little libraries that people build in their neighborhoods all over the world, or *Harris County Public Library* in Houston that pins a book of the day up on their board. American Libraries Magazine has an interesting assortment of boards that they regularly pin to, and the *Center for Transportation Research Library* in Austin, Texas, is all about showing how people get from point A to point B. Don't miss the fun of the *Awful Library Books* Pinterest boards featuring odd things found in the library; re-pin a couple of pins from this site and watch to see how fast your followers respond. Or follow *Public Libraries* magazine at http://www.pinterest.com/publibonline for more ideas for your boards. Some other ideas are:

- History photos and archives
- Promoting events
- Curate reading lists for special topics or ages
- Infographics from different learning-related topics
- Sharing new materials
- Learning materials for parents of preschoolers
- Book-related DIY craft projects
- How to run a book club board, with book ideas and discussion questions
- Curate a board of pins that your customers send you around a theme
- Since library vendors are also on Pinterest, look for promotional materials through NoveList, GoodReads, and more

Take original photos, and then overlay text and your avatar. An easy online image maker is Share As Image (http://www.shareasimage.com), which allows you to add text to images and share them over all of your channels. You can also add hashtags and comments to pins to increase your exposure.

## LINKEDIN

LinkedIn (http://www.linkedin.com) asks you to add a member profile page, which includes education, employment history, and a skills list. With the basic free membership, you can establish *connections* with other business professionals that you know or that know someone you know. As a social networking site for professional networking and the business community, many people only look to LinkedIn if they are trying to find a new job. But participating in LinkedIn Groups can be another great way of showing the community that the library is relevant. LinkedIn has been working on expanding their offerings for nonprofits. They now offer customizable business pages for nonprofits with "LinkedIn for Good" (https://nonprofits.linkedin.com), which focuses on nonprofit activities and features Board Connect, a program that helps nonprofits find people to join their boards as well as volunteer recruitment pages.

To use LinkedIn for the library, you need to build a personal profile first; then you can create your Company Page. This setup can cause problems if you leave your library, so be sure you assign an additional administrator who can take over if needed. To connect with businesses, offer them value, spark conversations, seek their opinions, or ask business leaders to guest blog on your site or to give presentations about National Entrepreneurs' Day or be interviewed in a podcast.

Join LinkedIn Groups and create your own group for your library to reach new audiences. You can browse the group categories by going to http://www.linkedin.com/directory/groups to see what groups are already formed. If you set up your own group, you can make it a private group so that people have to ask to join, or make it an open one so that anyone can take part. You could start your own group by a addressing a certain topic of interest that you have or that the library can respond to, such as Nonfiction Writers, or Scrabble Players, or eBook Readers Group, or a Business Database Users group. Follow other businesses in your community and make comments on their posts. Endorse others in your community—to get endorsements, you have to give them out!

## GOOGLE+

Everyone who sets up a Google email account is automatically given a Google+ account; one is built on the other. Google+ is a social networking channel much like Facebook, but instead of being reliant on the people and contacts you already have, Google+ helps you to build new contacts with people around communities and circles of interest themes. You join communities of people with like-minded interests, say other library lovers, then you can refine that community into circles, such as one for adults, one for kids. You can control the amount of content you see from your communities in your settings. Google+ tends to draw a male-dominated crowd because of a heavy emphasis on tech and gaming communities, and it doesn't currently have any advertising, frankly because it is owned by Google and they don't need it. As with LinkedIn, your business page is linked to your personal page. Create your library page as a nonprofit organization, so you can add nonprofit circles to watch what other libraries are doing. Look for other circles to join that have like-minded missions. You can tag other organizations by adding a plus symbol (+) in front of their handle name.

Unlike Facebook, as of this writing, all of your posts on Google+ can be seen by followers who have you in their circle, which also means your posts need to be extra impactful to be noticed. Upload your YouTube videos (another Google-owned channel) to your Google+ stream, or record them directly in Google+. All social networking sites are becoming more visual, so grab attention by doing a video on how to download an eBook or do a tour of the children's section, get the staff to sing a nursery rhyme song, or do a 30-second book review.

Google+ has grown more slowly than some of other social media channels, but it is a very powerful application, especially when you add in the Hangouts videoconferencing feature and the additional way to embed YouTube videos. Also, because it is a Google product, Google+ pages show up in Google searches and get priority placement in the images search especially if they have a lot of +1s. As of this writing, they are experimenting with an online giving feature, Google Wallet, which might become a huge asset for your Friends group as they join the social media bandwagon.

## SOCIAL MEDIA TEAM APPROACH

Many organizations use a team approach to their social media posts in order to spread the workload and gain perspectives from various experts. If you decide to take this approach, be sure to train your staff on the best practices along with pertinent policy issues, and how to organize for balanced coverage. Some libraries work straight off their editorial calendar and organize their work by week on a shared Excel spreadsheet. Each staff member takes a channel per week and is responsible for the content to be posted there. Theme days on the calendar can be helpful to drive content (e.g., Make a Change Monday, Throwback Thursday, Follow Friday). Some libraries assign each day to a different staff member; they are given specific parameters as to how many posts they should do, when they should schedule their posts to go up, branding guidelines for the post (i.e., how the library should be referenced), and ideas on content. If you use a team approach, talk to your team about having a cohesive voice, not that they can't add it to what their personal passions are; but all of the posts should look like they are coming from the same entity representing your brand.

**MOXIE TIP** Even if you are not ready to take the plunge into all of these social media channels, be sure to go into each one and sign up so that you can save your handle and URL name for the future before someone else claims it. Once someone else takes ownership of your name, it is impossible to get it back.

Once your social media avenues and goals are set, the next step is creating a marketing plan that incorporates best practices. Six months is a long time in social media; try to avoid looking online for specific practices older than this for reference. A media policy will direct who you want to be able to comment and respond to your posts. Set up notifications so you know when someone is commenting on your content—you will want to respond! Keep track of what topics are trending and what keeps coming up; should you address it? Keep your goals in mind to decide if advertising in Facebook is right for your library. Twitter is a great way to raise awareness quickly. Live tweet your event and invite others to tweet @ you! Be sure to add Twitter and Facebook links in your blogs and eNewsletters. YouTube is the next way to get your information out there. Topics can range from an informative how-to video to community news and external content. Be sure to link your YouTube channel to your other media channels! Instagram and Pinterest allow photos to be king, but be sure to label and describe your image as well so viewers know why you posted what you did, and don't forget the hashtags. LinkedIn and Google+ tend to run the more professional gambit. Create connections and circles that will in turn widen your audience. You don't have to do it all by yourself! Use your team to create content, brainstorm, and comment.

## REFERENCE

Walter, E. (2014). "The Best and Worst of Real-Time Marketing: 4 Lessons for Marketers." http://m.fastcompany.com/3031542/hit-the-ground-running/the-best-and-worst-of -real-time-marketing-4-lessons-for-marketers.

# 7

# OTHER NEW TECHNOLOGIES: VIDEO, QR CODES, AND MORE

## VIDEO

Lights, Camera, Action! Gone are the days when, if you wanted to have a video made, you needed to go to a producer who had the cameras, tripods, microphones, and a room full of mixing equipment; then you would have to buy airtime on a local TV channel; and, if you got lucky, you could find a sponsor to foot the bill. This was a tedious tale of scripting, producing, directing, editing, and adding final credits. Today's marketers get out their smartphones, press an app, and in six seconds, upload a video to all their social media channels. What started out as a rigorous, highly involved effort has now been simplified to the point that young children can and are producing video. But both types of video productions have their places in the marketing world we know.

It hasn't taken that long for things to change. In April 2005, technology pioneers Chad Hurley, Steve Chin, and Jawed Karin launched the age of the modern social media video when they loaded their first video to their new video-sharing website YouTube. In just 12 months, it went from 50,000 monthly users to 17 million. By 2006 more than 65,000 videos were being added daily. Suddenly, comics who never could get a break were online sensations; the zany adventures of peoples' cats made them stars; and marketing your business with video became easier and even more important. Today the word *viral* has a completely new meaning.

So how do libraries fit into this new realm of video and put it to good use? With everything that is currently out in cyberspace, where do you start?

- Remember that your community, however large or small, has a creative population that you can tap into.
- There are people in this world who LOVE being in front of a camera.

- Take a risk—you will never know what might take off as a success unless you try a lot of different things first.
- Don't overthink it! You have important information to get out there—clarify a marketing strategy that works in this visual platform.

Identify people in your community who love being on stage and start a list of their stage personalities, vocal attributes, and charisma. Use this list to help with brainstorming of your videos. A certain type of on-screen persona and charisma will make your online video presence come to life. Use this persona to define your library "style."

Don't forget the social side of online videos, whether it is YouTube, Vine, Instagram, or another channel. When people comment, with good, bad, or other comments, you will soon learn what information resonates with your community.

As far as SEO (Search Engine Optimization), which helps online searchers find your library, remember that you will benefit by exposure on YouTube, since Google indexes all the videos loaded. Many people use YouTube as a search engine to look up topics of interest, and you want your library to be on the search list!

## Traditional versus Instant Video

Not sure if video is for you? Start out slowly. Have fun! Use it to tell your library story through interviews or how-to highlights; be creative, and don't be boring. Check out online videos to see some creative ways to explain complicated information in a simplified format. Look for white board drawings speeded up, photographic slides with a voice-over, animation using paper cutouts, and more! Use videos to promote a special event and extend the reach to who might want to come. The University of Oregon used a video to promote their Edible Book Festival in 2010 (http://www.youtube.com/t11dUNVzxJs); then they could roll it out again to promote the 2011 festival.

Use video as a customer support tool to explain how to use services such as downloading books, rather than handing someone a 12-page booklet. Use video on your blog as an interview with an author or a book review done by a teen. Use video at events to highlight what your library offers the community. Have a library cat? Post videos of the cat during "Caterday" on Saturdays (yes, this is a real thing). Use them as part of your fundraising and advocacy-awareness efforts to tell your library story through testimonials. When I'm planning a video promotion, I add into my content creation calendar what type of video it will be, traditional or instant. Choosing what channel to support your video marketing strategy is as important as doing your video. Traditional video is made and edited with a digital camera—anything from a high-dollar, professional-grade camera to an instamatic-type video camera like a Flip; and more and more marketers are using the camera on a smartphone for this.

When using the traditional methods, remember that no matter what type of camera you use, you will probably need additional lighting and sound-capturing devices to make the video more professional. You will also need some type of editing software. There are many to choose from, depending on what your needs are and how much money you have to spend. The YouTube channel itself has some easy editing software associated with it; or, if you want to really get into it, you can purchase a software package such as professional-level Adobe Premiere. Do some research into the ease of use and cost. Don't get carried away with software that has all the bells and whistles if it will take you six months of training to get up to speed using it. You basically need something that gives you the visual and sound on two separate layers, so that you can boost levels independently, take out any "ummmms" and "awwwhhhss," and add in copyright-free music and titles. I have added some additional software ideas for video and audio editing in the last chapter of this book.

Do you still see video as more work than you can handle at the end of your busy day? Then hire it out. Check with local marketing companies to see who they recommend. Look at freelance websites that offer videographers. You might try GigSalad (http://www.gigsalad.com) or Fiverr (http://www.fiverr.com) to see who has good ratings for working with clients. Check with the local high school or college and see if they have students who need an internship or some extra cash.

Instant video can be anything that is produced with an app, by either a phone or a tablet. Here are just a few of the media application venues where you can post your videos:

- Instagram (http://www.instagram.com): Owned by Facebook, you can film up to 16-second videos that will directly load on both channels. Needs to be accessed through an app on a smartphone or tablet.

- YouTube (http://www.youtube.com): Owned by Google, you can use it to host your videos and as a social networking site. You can upload up to a 10-minute video for free and longer ones for a fee. Add links to the YouTube channel in your social media posts or embed the links in your website. Newer versions of YouTube have also added in overlays that can link to fundraising promotions. Be sure to fill out all of the tags and description information so that your videos are easily found. Can be used on a PC or through an app on a smartphone or tablet.

- Vine (https://vine.co): Owned by Twitter and one of the newest, it takes a six-second video that repeats itself in a loop sequence on the Vine or Twitter channels or can be added to your Facebook page. Can be used through an app on a smartphone or tablet.

- Vimeo (http://www.vimeo.com): Founded by a group of filmmakers, this video-sharing site features more of the indie-type films for viewing. Check out the impressive comparison of video-hosting services on Wikipedia for more service information. Can be used on a PC or through an app on a smartphone or tablet.

- Animoto (http://www.animoto.com): Allows you to make a video from uploaded still photographs. It adds the music the animation, and POOF!—you have a professional-looking video to upload to other channels. This is a computer-based application.

Most of these channels enable instant uploading to the Internet as long as you have high-speed wireless or a strong cell signal. Some also allow you to save your videos to put online later so they will fit into your content calendar. These apps keep getting better and better, and easier to use. As with the traditional video, if you have the choice between paying for a better camera and paying for an additional microphone, go with the microphone. The cameras that are built into cell phones are amazing, but the mics are still so-so. People will forgive you for a shaking picture, but if they cannot hear the words, they will turn it off. Additional video and audio files do take up added space on the hard drives of your digital devices, so be sure and delete those that you will never use again!

A good example of using video to market a library service is the video "Interlibrary Loan Whiteboard" (http://www.youtube.com/watch?v=89eetuA5xP8), produced by the

Harold B. Lee Library. When using video to market a service, remember to hit the highlights, make it short, and make it engaging. Remember to go back to your marketing plan objectives to decide how the video will fit into your marketing strategies. Is it to educate, to show an event, to drive an increase in a service or to tell your library story and engage your customers? The next big wave of social media is video—the shorter, the better. Showing how to use one of your online databases in two minutes will trump the hour class that you offer every time!

## LIVESTREAMING VIDEO

Using a livestream as a communications channel is an expanding use of video. It might not be your go-to channel to get the word out on your library, but in certain circumstances, the knowledge will help to set you apart from other organizations in town. By using a livestream video, you might help promote a new library service where people can call in and get their library questions answered. You might use it for community programming by having a debate on a community topic. Reinforce your library's message by streaming an author visit where people can call in or tweet in their questions.

Thanks to inexpensive equipment and new technologies, livestreaming is becoming an accessible tool for your communication strategies. YouTube Live, Google+ Hangouts, Livestream (http://www.livestream.com), and Ustream (http://www.ustream.tv) are just a few of the many services that you can use to create a show and set up an online video channel. Many of these hosting services also allow you to set up a live chat with your audience. Or you can also use a Twitter hashtag code to have participants ask questions. Live video is a great way to get internal marketing information out to staff in different buildings. Instead of everyone having to drive across town to a meeting, directors and managers can host a morning meeting for five minutes to everyone in their system. If you already have the equipment to do video work, offering livestreaming is basically connecting that to a streaming provider. If you are looking for ways to market your programs and services to a larger geographic area, or you have barriers to people coming to a popular program such as not enough seats, or if you have a high demographic of seniors in retirement facilities, broadcasting your author program can extend your reach and get people involved and excited about library programs and services that they can use at home. If seating is a problem, hold the event in one building and set up viewings in the other branches. This gets more people into the library as well as keeps the excitement going for a "one-night-only" event. Leveraging technology to extend your community reach will put you in a unique position to gain new customers.

## WEBINARS

An out-of-the-box way that you can be your own best advocate is by producing webinars for your internal and external audiences. Webinars are also a type of video streaming, but they have more of an educational foundation instead of an entertainment background. Everyone is familiar with webinars as a means of education about a certain topic, but the beauty of a webinar is that you can also market library collections, programs, and events remotely. Having a prepared slideshow and recorded audio can give you a tool for highlighting your library or staff member as an expert in a certain field, helping it to gain credibility as a relevant organization in the community. You can also gain community approval by using it as more of a town hall meeting for a remote focus group, by asking questions and having people respond via the chat function.

 **MOXIE TIP** What sort of broadband access does your community have? There is no point in doing a webinar if the people you are trying to reach cannot access it. If you live in a remote area or if Internet accessibility is sketchy, you may want to do the webinar as a taped presentation and load it onto a video channel for people to access rather than trying to do it live. If you are trying to increase the use of digital literacy in your community, do a webinar inside your library—you can be in a separate room and be seen through a laptop and projector in the other room. No one will know!

Managing successful webinars are a bit like having twin toddlers—you need to have several extra hands to do it right and not lose your mind. There are many platforms that you can use for webinars, and while the costs can be exorbitant for a small library—hundreds of dollars a month—I've found in my research that, many times, you really do get what you pay for. If you are just going for the quick-and-dirty version of getting the information out there, Google+ Hangouts might work just fine. If you want to do a series of professional webinars for community training purposes, you might look into various other webinar services such as GoToMeeting (http://www.gotomeeting.com) or Cisco WebEx. The following list will help in organizing your event and in deciding which system is best for you.

- Identify the topic and the speaker. Give them at least two months to plan the event.
- Write a summary of the event as well as how it fits into your strategic plan or marketing goals. You will probably need this in order to show validity for spending the extra money on the hosting. You will also use the summary information as a starting point for your promotions around the event.
- Choose your webinar platform. In choosing, don't just look at cost (even though that is the driver many times), but decide on your needs for the event.
  - How many people do you want to be able to attend, and how will they register?
  - Do you need a private chat feature, or will you be using a hashtag chat?
  - Will participants need to be able to send in questions?
  - Will the participants need to download an app or program to their computer in order to participate?
  - Do you want them to be able to access the webinar from a mobile device?
  - Do you want to be able to record the webinar for future availability?
  - Do you want customizable branding to be seen on the screen by your attendees?
  - Do you want to offer a polling feature to your presentation?
  - Is the platform a screen-sharing service, or can you embed video or a webcam?
  - How is the audio shared? Through the computer speakers, or from a call-in phone number?
  - Do the attendees get a reminder email, or can they get it added onto their online calendar?
  - What sort of technical support do they offer? There is nothing worse than 100 or 1,000 people waiting for the audio to come up!

- Build the webinar landing page on your website where your potential attendees can go to find out all about it and register. Make sure it is optimized for search engines.

- Script out the social media campaign on your content calendar. Make sure your posts are sharable so that everyone will hear about it!

- Build your webinar slides and script.

- Give all the information to a copresenter. This person will be in charge of the behind-the-scene details that you will need during the event, such as helping with sound check, moderating the incoming questions, helping with technical issues, sending out messages about specific resources, and watching the dashboard for any problems.

## PODCASTS

If you think of your library communications plan as being in the center or hub of the overall communications of your community, you can then begin to think about how these other technologies might fit in. Because we can no longer totally rely on the local media (newspapers, radio, television, etc.) to help us get the word out about the library, you need to think of the library as being its own broadcaster. Instead of paying to have a direct mail piece mailed to everyone in your district, look into other ways to reach your audience and try them out to see what resonates.

Marketers are always looking for new ways to reach people, in new ways that they want to be reached. Podcasts are a fun, easy way to reach out to your community. Merriam-Webster defines *podcast* as an audio program (music or talk) made available in digital format for automatic download over the Internet. Podcasts give you a way to diversify your content from strictly visual media channels by adding in audio. Podcasts can be put together quickly and can easily be used to record conversations with authors, share ideas from local experts, and explain how to use a new service or review books.

 **MOXIE TIP** Podcasts can be a little tricky to market. They don't engage a wide variety of users to download them specifically unless the topic is of interest to a broad range of people who are also tech savvy. Consider adding a poll to your blog post to see how many of your users listen to podcasts before adding them to your mix of channels. Podcasts can be used successfully as part of your blogging content or for a special series that would draw your customers to listen.

To produce a podcast, you will first need to acquire audio-recording and editing software. Check out Audacity (http://www.audacity.sourceforge.net) or look into Behringer PODCASTUDIO USB, which includes a full-recording studio "out of the box," including USB audio interface, mixer, microphone, headphones, and professional audio software. If you would rather piece it together, besides the software, you will need a way to convert your audio into an MP3 format and a good audio microphone. Decide if you would like a wireless lavaliere mic for people who like to walk while they talk, or a mic that would sit on a desk or podium. Products are discontinued so often that I won't give specific examples; but you might check out the blog *The Podcaster's Studio* (http://www.thepodcastersstudio .com), which has a podcast gear section to get you started.

Add podcasts to your blog posts along with a transcribed version to generate more written content for your site that can be searched. A good length for a podcast is two to six minutes long. You can additionally break up longer podcasts into multiple posts for a series.

## QUICK RESPONSE (QR) CODES

The QR code is a marketing phenomenon that gained wide popularity, but because every marketer jumped in and started using it badly, its reputation is failing. This little square of information is basically a URL address that you can scan with a reader app on a smartphone, which then takes you directly to the URL website. The good thing about using QR codes in your marketing activities is that it is an easy way to give added content to the person scanning it. These squares of code can be used to great advantage if used correctly. The bad thing about using them is that they may have been overused inappropriately, so most people won't take the time to scan it in. For example, a bad use of the QR codes has been posted on highway billboards. Really? Do they expect a person to stop on the highway, get out their phone, scan in a QR code, and then drive on? Not a good idea.

However, in some specialized cases, these codes can be used to the full advantage of what they were intended for. For example, we use a "shelf-talker" sign in the stacks to alert people that the nonfiction area they are browsing in also has information that can be found in our online database resources. The QR code takes them directly to the related database, instead of providing an address that they have to type in. For example, if they are browsing the U.S. history section, the QR code on the shelf talker would take them to the Academic Search Premier database for articles on U.S. history. QR codes can also be used sparingly on printed materials—for example, if you have value-added content such as a video of a musician you are promoting on a print flyer. Or you may want to link from a print notice to additional information about a contest. When using QR codes, be sure that they take your customers to interesting value-added content, rather just taking them to your main website.

In order to set up a QR code, identify the webpage you want to link to, then paste the URL of that webpage into a QR code generator, like QR Stuff (http://www.qrstuff.com) or QR Code Monkey (http://www.qrcode-monkey.com). These programs allow you to add in color, your logo and other fun stuff. Download the QR code graphic that the program generates, and insert or paste it onto the flier or poster.

The most important step in using a QR code is to make sure that you let the person viewing the code know that there is extra content available by accessing it, as well the second important step of setting up the analytics on the page that the code goes to, so that you can track how many times the code has been used to access that page. This will help you find out if this has been a worthwhile endeavor that your community responds to, or just more work on your part that no one cares about.

## DOCUMENT SHARING

One of the latest trends in online information-sharing is slide or presentation hosting services. These are online sites where you can upload your PowerPoint presentation for viewing or use the hosting service such as Haiku Deck (http://www.Haikudeck.com), or Prezi (http://www.prezi.com) to create the presentation first and then share it. These sites let you view and comment on others' slideshows. There are more and more to choose from, such as SlideBoom (http://www.slideboom.com) and SlideShare (http://www.slideshare .net), the latter being one of the most popular. These sites are basically a social website built around documents. An uploaded PowerPoint presentation can be shared, discussed, and seen by thousands of people. Use this as a way to get out the information from your annual report, or details on why the community needs to vote on a tax increase for your library. You can make these documents available for downloading, or they can be hosted on SlideShare and embedded on your website or blog. Go to SlideShare to view informative presentations like "Libraries as Microcelebrities" by Pecha Kucha, or "Get Over Yourself! Improving Your Library's Online Presence" by Laura Solomon, or learn how to borrow a living book at the Pickering Public Library, "Living Library Event" by Anna-Marie McDonald, which as of this writing had 32,000 views!

## HASHTAGS

Hashtags are an easy, fun way to engage your social audiences in side chats during a library promotion, or to use them with staff to do quick surveys during staff presentations. I have used them to help answer specific questions about library services and in promotions during #NationalLibraryWeek and #GeekTheLibrary. Many people associate hashtags only with Twitter, but they are widely used through other social networks such as Instagram, Facebook, and YouTube as a way to do searches for content and events, and to find others who are having conversations about the things you are interested in. Using a hashtag in a post makes the phrase a clickable link and will make your content easier for others to find. To search for hashtags in Facebook, go to http://www.facebook.com/hashtag/XXX (replace the x's with the hashtag you are looking up). Each hashtag on Facebook has its own unique URL with a status update box (currently this is only available when working through the Internet site, not by the mobile app).

Hashtags can help you gauge interest in programs or services that you might want to bring to your library. You can start or join conversations by placing the "#" symbol before a keyword in a tweet or other channel. This generates a live feed that adds your message to others that have used the same hashtag. If you want to start a new conversation with your community, go to Hashtags.org (http://www.hashtags.org), or do a Twitter search to see if the keyword you want to use is already in use. You will need a Twitter account, and it is handy to also use a third-party aggregator application such as Hootsuite (http://www .hootsuite.com) or TweetDeck (http://www.tweetdeck.com) so that you can monitor your hashtag in its own column.

Always have someone else proof and double-check your hashtags before you use them. As you might see, having several words that run together might lead to it being read in different ways by different people, such as #nowthatchersdead. Is that meant to say "Now Thatcher's Dead," referring to the death of Prime Minister Margaret Thatcher, or is this being read "Now That Cher's Dead" referring to the surprised pop singer? (Crossfield 2014).

Use your hashtag on posters and posts to get the tag into the social conversation. There are some wonderful resources out there to help you use hashtags to their fullest. Look at Content Marketing Institute's #Hashtagology 101 (Crossfield 2014), or do some research and find a local expert to set you up! Another way to involve people in conversations is to do a search for similar-interest hashtags, such as #artist if you are planning an artist reception or movie night about Van Gogh; you can join the #artist conversation and use your own hashtag in your retweets or response to other tweets. Just don't go crazy with hashtags—two or three at the most is all you need to add; otherwise, you might be seen as a hashtag spammer. Once you begin seeing your hashtag tweets being replied to and retweeted, you will be amazed at the interesting conversations they bring up!

Many people in the field consider the term *marketing* to mean a one-way flow of information. A better term would be *communication*, which infers more of a two-way conversation. However, rather than getting bogged down in lots of terminology, just be sure you put your creative talents to work and are successful! Whatever technology you use for your communications, new or old, test what works for you in your situation, and don't be afraid to take a risk and try something new. Even if your analysis at the end shows that it wasn't a hit, in six months, your customers may be ready for the new technology, and you will be the expert!

New technologies just like social media are changing constantly. Try branching out of your website and newsletter box by trying more frequent communications in multiple places. Use your community to find video personalities. When you have begun posting your videos, pay attention to the comments. You will quickly learn the good and bad of what you are posting. Traditional methods of filming can be time consuming, but with the right equipment, a high-quality video can really make an impression. You can always hire someone else, too! Instant video created by using an app can be used in many applications and on many sites. Don't forget, the shorter, the better! Video communicates to a broad audience and is more affordable than ever, and as a visual and creative marketing tool, it can't be beat. Livestreaming and webinars create instant contact with your customers—whether informative, educational, or entertaining, you are getting to your one-on-one relationship! QR codes can be great for internal marketing, but make sure they link to content your customer actually wants, not something you think they need. Placement is important, and don't overuse! Sharing document sites can be useful for more in-depth documents like your annual report or presentations about an event.

## REFERENCE

Crossfield, J. (2014). *#Hashtagology 101: How to Use Hashtags in Your Social Media Content.* http://contentmarketinginstitute.com/2014/02/hashtags-social-media-content.

# 8

# ADVOCACY AND FUNDRAISING

Now more than ever, library marketers are being asked not to only make sure that there are people in the seats at programs, but also that they become library supporters by voting for libraries in the next election or contributing money to a new building campaign. Growing and engaging supporters is the ultimate job of a marketer. Whether you are asked to help set up a fundraising and/or marketing program for your library, or you are asked to consult with your Friends group to help them plan the next big campaign, you will be the best person to roll out the strategic best practices for communications outreach for your customers.

In a world where libraries continue to experience declining budgets, advocacy and fundraising are increasingly brought up as worthwhile endeavors. In generations past, the local Friends of the Library group was the savior of many a summer reading program or author visit. With today's reality, Friends groups and library foundations are being asked to do more and more. Many times these groups are made up of lifelong library lovers who have a passion to see library services in a democratic society and want that to continue for the next generation. There are Friends groups nationally that raise millions of dollars to build new buildings, to maintain special programming or just to keep the lights on. Our philanthropic library organizations are part of who we are and how we operate. As a library marketer, you should be working hand in hand with them in order to make sure not only that they are as successful as they can be, but also that the messages that both organizations are sending out to the public are not at odds.

Local library boards, Friends groups, and foundation boards are the keys to your calls to advocate for not closing buildings and mill levy hikes, as well as the needed changes of taking your quiet reading area and turning it into a noisy makerspace for teens. Your community goes to them with questions and thoughts about the library, and it uses members as messaging channels. It only makes sense that these members be kept up to date with the communications channels and marketing tactics the library is using.

Invite board members to be part of your marketing plan. Ask them to write guest blog posts and opinion pieces for the newspaper, to be a copresenter for a webinar, or to do a six-second recorded book review for Vine. Add them into your marketing plan, not only to give you great new content, but also to train them on how their advocacy relates to your marketing. These people are at the highest points in your community engagement strategies, and if they are busy businesspeople or retirees planning their next beach vacation, they might not be social media users or might not understand the changing demographics of philanthropy, so training may also be needed.

Part of library advocacy includes demonstrating the need for libraries to the next generation as well as showing them how they can help. Libraries need new, younger volunteers for their philanthropic initiatives. Furthermore, the shift from the stereotypical library volunteer as a stay-at-home mom looking for outside stimulation to the person who has just been downsized from their company and is looking to gain new work skills is a reality.

Changes in generational attitudes toward philanthropy are being studied by many nonprofit organizations. Where the older generation saw volunteering as giving back and a community duty, the Generation Y (those in the 22–32 age bracket) see themselves as part of the larger world. They are more likely to give money to an African cause for clean water than to give time or talent to help their local library. Perhaps this is because libraries do a poor job of marketing their services and offerings compared to other nonprofits.

Look at your marketing plan and ask yourself how many of your efforts go to any sort of fundraising or library advocacy efforts. Until the library doors are going to be padlocked shut, the communications going out will likely be "Check out the latest best seller" or "We have free Internet." These aren't the issues that keep you awake at night, and there is so much more to libraries. Will libraries still be around in the next 20 or 50 years? This is the crucial point to everything that you do every day—how will libraries change to fit the needs of the coming generations and stay relevant to them?

As you do your market research on best practices of marketing to different demographic segments, keep an eye on information pertaining to trends for donating with different generations. Check out the Association of Fundraising Professionals (http://www.afpnet.org), or look toward your local United Way. Our library is part of the Foundation Center online (http://www.foundationcenter.org), where you can find a wealth of information such as in-depth grant maker profiles, a grant database, instruction on funding research, and help with proposal writing. Your library or a library near you also might have access to databases such as Grantspace.org, Philanthropy In/Sight, Grants.gov, and other research tools for grants.

If your library foundation has a paid staff member to manage development and fundraising activities, your goals are aligned in that you both want new customers/donors, you both want higher levels of community engagement, and you both see the need for multichannel communications to reach people where they are. Also, you are both producing content—your counterpart might be reaching out in a more traditional means through direct mail, while you might be doing podcasts. He or she might be looking at short-term fundraising for purchasing new library computers, while you work on the long-term marketing strategy that goes along with the computers. Needless to say, you need to work together and make sure you are putting out consistent messages.

Some of the newer fundraising tools to go along with the tried-and-true direct mail piece are of course aligned with social networks and online donation systems. It will be worthwhile for you to be familiar with these tools when the call goes out, "We need money!"

## CROWD FUNDING

This new fundraising tool has blown into our lives with fervor in the last couple of years. Whether it is a Kickstarter (http://www.kickstarter.com) campaign for a local band to buy new instruments or a statewide charitable giving campaign like Giving Tuesday, this type of fundraising effort is multiplying as fast as the ways people are using it. Crowd funding is defined as a fundraising effort where individuals are brought together to finance a cause, and it is usually highlighted by those crowds of individuals giving typically smaller donation amounts through an online service. Many times these crowd-funding campaigns are used as a tactic to get money for an emergency situation within a limited period. A sense of urgency and requests for donations of small amounts of money from large amounts of people drive these fundraising efforts.

People love to share what they are excited about through their social networks, and if they can share the library cause that you are raising funds for, this wins for you not only in driving new donors to the library, but also in increased awareness for the library as a place that needs donations. Most of the crowd-funding sites have a vetting process, and specific parameters for what types of efforts they will fund. Kickstarter is one of the most talked-about sites where creative projects are more the norm. They don't do businesses, causes, or charities; but if you are looking for a mural for your building or video equipment for your new makerspace, this might be the place to try. Another crowd funding site is Indiegogo (http://www.indiegogo.com), which will approve fundraising campaigns for almost anything. In looking at the site I have seen many efforts to fund homemade "Little Free Libraries" as well as fundraising efforts to build a library in Juneau, Alaska, by selling bricks with Harry Potter character names on them as a tribute wall. An interesting campaign that was funded was "The Liberty Ride," by the Friends of the Somerville Public Library in Massachusetts. This campaign was to raise money to hold a bike tour through Somerville to each of the three branch libraries. A celebration of mind and body, money raised would be to install permanent bike air pumps at the libraries. Their goal was $500, and they reached $770 with 44 funders.

Some other funding sites you may look at are RocketHub (http://www.rockethub.com), which connects creative projects with potential promotion and marketing partners. Looking to fund a new mobile app for your library? Look into appbackr (http://www.appbackr .com). There are more of these coming out every year, and we have a local community-based crowd-funding source called Community Funded (http://www.communityfunded .com), which helps local organizations and funders connect. Whichever of these you might choose, remember that getting the word out on these crowd-funding sites are social media–based, so if you haven't ramped up the moxie on your social media channels, these may not be the way to go.

Community nonprofit organizations have banded together to work on days of giving. Look up Give Local America (http://www.givelocalamerica.org), or use the hashtag #GivingDay, or search for @GiveLocal where you can do social media searches to see who might be doing it in your state. Successful marketing strategies should include:

- Sharing the goals of what you are going to do with the money
- Focusing on your library's mission and how you help the community

- Showing how people can share the word about your mission and goals through creative pieces that they will happily share with their friends
- Recognizing donors or people interested in making a challenge grant to get things going at the beginning or ramp it up for a last push

## TEXT TO GIVE

Using a cell phone with texting ability, this mobile fundraising tool is something almost anyone can use. The donation will show up on your mobile phone bill. This tool provides a quick and easy way to build momentum for a giving campaign as well as reinforce your messages delivered through your other fundraising channels. This tool has been especially effective when used for emergency earthquake and tornado relief by the American Red Cross. Nonprofits such as libraries and Friends organizations can use this instant support technique to rally supporters for a giving campaign around capital improvements, summer reading program enhancements, funding author visits or one-book campaigns to buy everyone the same book to read. One of the fun aspects is that you could flash the text word up on the screen during a video program or a live program as well as add it to all your social media links.

Text-to-give technology is still fairly expensive to use for a small library, but for the larger systems that would be able to have the funds to pay for the startup fee and monthly rates, this might be a great tool to add into your fundraising mix. Text to give is becoming more popular and some of the costs are coming down, so it is worth some research to see if it might work for you, especially if you have an urgent need for money for an emergency situation. Check out the Mobile Giving Foundation (http://www.mobilegiving.org), which provides organizational elements to charities who want to use text to give campaigns. Some others are mGive (http://www.mgive.com) and MobileCause (http://www.mobilecause.com. A few of the mobile giving technologies through texting or apps are Text2Give, GivebyCell, Hipcricket, and Connect2Give. This new fundraising application is definitely the next big wave, so get your surfboard out and jump on!

## WEBSITE DONATIONS

Even if your job responsibilities don't include fundraising activities, they probably include managing website content. Because any giving activities done through social media channels refer people back to the website (or should), consider how these pieces come together. If you don't have a fundraising campaign going on right now, consider adding a donation link to your website, even if only as an awareness effort. You can use a web-based donation system such as PayPal (http://www.paypal.com), which gives a discount on their fees to nonprofits to have people actually donate online. There are many to choose from—for example, Network for Good's Donate Now system, Click & Pledge, and more. All of the systems take a small processing fee per donation and have various ways of sending you back the proceeds; some send you a monthly check, and some wait until the donations are up to a certain amount before they disperse the money. Either way, they are an easy way to get donations throughout the year or for a particular ask event such as a building campaign or a new technology campaign. Use your blog and/or website as the hub for all of your activities. It doesn't make sense to have a separate site for charitable giving. Make it as easy as possible for people to give the library money!

## INCREASING DONATIONS WITH SOCIAL MEDIA

The number of new social networking tools expands daily (or even hourly). Keeping track of the newest tools, and thinking about how they might work for your library, can be a full-time job. Look at attending some webinars, often for free, through organizations such as Network for Good (http://www.networkforgood.org), the Chronicle of Philanthropy, Greater Giving, Nonprofit Hub, and Charity How To. Sponsor a quarterly nonprofit fundraising group at the library to share ideas and look for collaborations with other local nonprofits. Sign up for nonprofit marketing groups through LinkedIn such as Marketing Public Libraries Think Tank, PR Professionals, Social Media for Nonprofit Organizations, and Social Media Marketing. Also, anytime you download a white paper or attend a webinar, you will likely get put onto an email list by those savvy marketers. I have set up a separate email account to use just for this case so these sometimes daily emails aren't mixed into my regular work feed.

If you hear of a successful social media fundraising campaign, such as the very successful ALS Ice Bucket Challenge, do some digging and find out who was in charge of it. Call them up and ask questions. People always like to talk about their successes.

**Some Great Fundraising Ideas to Look at Include:**

MOXIE TIP

- Tweetathons—create a unique hashtag around a cause, then drive people with your outstanding content to your website to donate. For a good resource on how to do this, go to http://shonaliburke.com/2012/01/11/12-tips-to-organize-and-run-a-tweetathon.

- A retweet sponsorship—a cause-marketing partner tweet campaign, such as they pay you a dollar for every retweet that goes out that has their hashtag in it. Check out RT2Give (https://twitter.com/rt2give).

- Do some research on how you can collaborate with TechSoup for Libraries (http://www.techsoupforlibraries.org) to see if you are eligible for software and hardware product donations and learning resources. They also hold webinars and forums on various tech topics.

- Create a YouTube video for your fundraising message with an added overlay showing a dollar bill and asking for a donation. YouTube has clickable annotations that are embedded in the video that nonprofit organizations can link their donation page or volunteer sign up pages to. This needs to be set up through YouTube's Nonprofit Program. Go to http://www.youtube.com/nonprofits to see how you can add a donate button, a call-to-action overlay, or video annotations.

- Keep an eye on Facebook and some of the other big players who are experimenting with fundraising properties built into their system.

## DIRECT MAIL

People often overlook the positives of direct mail, mainly because of the rising costs of postage. Sending a direct mail piece still produces one of the highest rates of return, especially in terms of fundraising. Get creative with postcards to help save on postage, as well as guarantee that your message will be read and won't be tossed before it is opened. Check with the post office to find out the largest size you can mail and still get a postcard rate.

Look for a direct mail center who, for as small as a penny a piece, will auto-address your pieces using your mailing list. Costs for direct mail are always cheaper per piece the more you send out, so think about bulking up your mailing by buying a targeted demographic list or using a zip code search for a list.

Here are some tips to use in preparing direct mail content:

- Use a conversational style and focus on the reader
- Some samples of opening lines might include: "If you're like me. . .," "You are our. . .," or "You are invited. . ."
- Keep the sentences short for enhanced readability.
- Keep the first paragraph to three lines or less.
- If you can't think of that wonderful opening line, just start writing and it will come to you as you write.
- Keep the content short; in our world of information overload, people will usually read the first two paragraphs and then skip to the bottom, if you can get them that far, you have done a pretty good job. If you can get them to take the called-for action, you have done a wonderful job!
- If you need to do a direct mail piece with an enclosed return envelope or other piece, pay the extra to have an outer envelope teaser statement printed to encourage people to open the envelope.
- Create interest with an unexpected number or percentage, such as "24.6% of Libraries. . .," in the headline.

Have your letter or postcard designed and printed professionally, using bold headlines, bright colors, and beautiful photos and graphics. If you do a postcard, keep a corner on the back blank for your personalized message, like "It was great seeing you at the event last year—I hope you can come again!" If you don't have an inexpensive printer in your area, look for online printers such as Postcards.com, who do printing and mailing services. Log onto your Pinterest account and search for "Direct Mail Examples" or "Creative Direct Mail" to see noteworthy examples of postcards as well as creative direct mail ideas that you can repurpose for your library.

## COMMUNITY PARTNERSHIPS

Working with community partners is a type of advocacy effort that everyone should be working to foster. Libraries often get many, many calls from business who want to *partner*. These partners can be anything from "Can I give out ice cream coupons to all your story-time kids?" to "We are having a volunteer day, have you got things that 50 of us can do?" Partnerships with local businesses and community organizations can be a great way to build on community relationships, if you start them the right way. The latest trend in many businesses marketing plans is *cause* marketing. Businesses are looking for worthy, socially responsible companies to align themselves with—the library should be one of those! Businesses want to connect and resonate with their customers just like nonprofits do. The first step is making it known that you are looking for business partnerships—go to other non-profit fundraisers, talk to other local marketing people, make sure that libraries are seen as collaborative businesses and that their influence is a good match for certain businesses. Businesses want to be involved in local events, and many are beginning to invest in their own grant giving–associated nonprofits as part of their business model. Many businesses use these creative cause campaigns as part of their word-of-mouth strategy. For example, "Come out and see the Habitat for Humanity's house that our employees built."

As part of your marketing strategy, make a list of local companies that you could team up with. The biggest part is making sure that the collaboration becomes a true win for both parties. When meeting with a business, be frank about asking what their needs are and about telling them what the library needs. If the two sets of needs don't align, that's okay. Just say thank you and move on. Don't fall into the trap of giving up your needs for an additional money donation knowing that you will be spending more hours organizing an event —it is not worth it in the long run!

The cross-promotion that can be generated from a planned campaign will go way beyond what either of the parties could do on their own. Our town is filled with microbreweries, and along with that comes a certain amount of angst from locals that the beer business is taking over the town. But look at them as part of the culture of the community, whether you believe in drinking beer or not. They are small businesses looking for nonprofits to do cause marketing with. So how can you make it a win-win?

- Host a "Books and Brew" night with an author of a DYI brew guide.
- Highlight beer materials during the annual brew festival, in the library and at the brewpubs.
- Send a staff person to the Geeks Who Drink Meetup, to highlight where to find all the great trivia data they need.
- Ask the local brewer to name a seasonal brew after your library.
- Run a joint campaign with the brewer of some sort where your customers might need to sign up to get a free beer; then you can turn those signups into a mailing list that you could both use.
- Ask the beer trucks to deliver library materials to nursing homes.
- Host an adult spelling bee at one of the brewpubs to engage new audiences who might not be library users.

These are the types of WOMM campaigns that don't cost a lot of money, but make libraries seem relevant and part of the community. Businesses that want to give you money and not do any of the work are not *partnerships*; these are *sponsorships*. There is also a place for those in the world of ever-shrinking library budgets, but be sure which one you are really signing up for, and signing up means getting it in writing. Put into writing your expectations, their expectations, each other's deliverables, timeline, and other details.

## SPONSORSHIPS

Libraries are somewhat accustomed to the idea of sponsorship because most have a Friends group or a foundation that serves as a sponsor by raising money to give to the library. However, not as many libraries are used to the idea of a business being a sponsor, and what making a winning relationship for both parties entails.

Businesses know that their local library has a positive connection with their customers and the community at large. In this business-to-business (B2B) transaction, the partnership must benefit both parties. In a world where people are bombarded with advertising every minute, many library boards and managers are reluctant to bring advertising into the library. There is also the concern that if one business is seen over others, somehow the library is promoting that business. But, if handled well, sponsorship does not necessarily mean that the library will become overly commercialized. Furthermore, staff and public need to understand that in these days of shrinking library budgets, business sponsorships can be welcome and successful additions to your marketing strategies.

When embarking on a sponsorship plan, the first thing to do is make sure that you have a sponsorship policy in place. If you are part of an academic organization or city government, you probably already have one. If you need to write one, ask your peer libraries to supply copies of theirs for you to review as a starting point. The American Library Association through their Trustee Division has put up a sample Sponsorship/Partnership Policies (along with some other types of sample policies) on their website for libraries to use a starting place; you can view it at http://www.ala.org/united/trustees/orgtools/policies. Some points in your policy to consider would include:

- Will you give branded items from sponsors to your customers, such as bookmarks, key chains, etc.?
- What control are you willing to give away as far as naming rights—not only for physical items such as park benches and rooms, but also programs and collections?

Sponsorship procedural items might include a sample of the written letter of agreement, which includes:

- What each of you is agreeing to
- Dates or deadlines for any of the promotional activities
- Invoicing and payment schedules

If your relationship covers an extended time, you may want to add in an escape clause. You may need an out if, for instance, they go out of business, or if something happens and you perceive them as reflecting negatively on the library.

The first step to creating a sponsorship policy is figuring out what your library is worth in terms of marketing value. Say you have 10,000 views of your website a day, and 1,000 people walk through your doors, and you print 5,000 newsletters that are picked up—each of these points can be seen by a sponsor as a media exposure, and you should be able to put a monetary value on each of them. If you don't have the faintest idea about what value to give your own media exposure markets, look at advertising rates for your local newspaper or radio station. They have your media market broken down to a science by how many page views per how many people correspond to how much the advertising should cost.

Don't sell yourself short! In the 1970s, our library system sold naming rights to a room in the building for $5,000. At the time, I'm sure that they were so thankful to have any type of donation that it didn't occur to them that this room would have that name for the next 40 years. The sponsor got a great deal! But when the inside of the library was remodeled, and that room went away, so did the recognition. So be sure to have a policy in place about a time limit on sponsorships where they can either be renegotiated or dropped.

Many sponsors who cater to young families are interested in sponsoring summer reading programs. Make a list of all of the media exposure points where a sponsor logo might be seen, and put a cost on it. Have a sponsorship levels document already set up that you can use year to year. For example, for $200, the sponsor gets their name announced at a program, and they are allowed to give away coupons to the participants. For $500, they get their name put on the summer reading information that is sent out to 20,000 school-age kids. You get the idea; go up from there to the $10,000-and-up sponsorships. Having everything already spelled out not only helps you with negotiating sponsorships, but it makes it look like more of a business-to-business (or B2B in the new trending slang) transaction and increases the likelihood of successful relationships.

Another part of your negotiations with potential sponsors is how the money can be given. Can the business give you a single check for the full amount, or do they need to break it up into monthly payments over a year? Make sure you have a procedure in place through your purchasing department for invoicing and billing sponsors, so that you don't have to become the purchasing agent also.

Once you have your letter of agreement signed, make sure that anyone involved in fulfilling the agreement is notified. For example, the graphic designer needs to put the sponsor's logo on all the program materials; the web developer needs to know where to put the website link, etc. It is your job to communicate regularly with your contact and to send reports on how the sponsorship is going and what their money is being used for. Adding in statistics like attendance at the program, how many items were given out with their logo on it, etc., is the best way to keep the relationship positive and let them know that the library is a good investment.

A library marketer must work closely with the Friends of the Library and the foundation. Making sure your messages match and your branding is consistent is a must. Inviting board members to be a part of the marketing plan is one way to keep communication up. Make them aware that they have an important role to play in marketing. Both you and the board should be aware of generational changes and how they can affect your philanthropic efforts. Crowd funding is a new wave of fundraising. Through certain sites fundraising efforts can be amplified. Keep in mind the specifics of your goals when choosing a site as well as when planning your marketing. Text to give, website fundraising, social media, and direct mail are all tactics for getting the money. Make sure the channel you use is appropriate for the audience you are trying to attract to your message and therefore donate. Look for community partners. These partners can provide not only volunteers, but also valuable marketing in the community. If you have businesses that just want to donate, they will likely fall into the sponsorship category. A sponsorship policy will help to narrow the types of businesses you want to take money from as well as guaranteeing your library won't become overly commercialized.

# TOOLBOX TIDBITS

## MARKETING LANGUAGE CACHE

To save time, add emphasis, and spark creativity, spend the time up front to put together a marketing language cache. This cache, or stockpile, of your marketing resources is a must-have not only for you, but for marketing deputies in your organization who are constantly calling you to send them a logo, a marketing document, or a photo of the building. Having a one-stop cache of materials will help you when you are stuck for a tagline, looking for ideas for your blog, or giving staff their talking points or elevator speech for a new service.

You can put together your cache in whatever system works for you. You can have folders in your email system, or a file with folders on a shared server, so all staff can access them. Add stories and quotes to your language cache. When staff send you those tidbits of what someone said to them or what happened at a program (both good and bad), capture that information and file it away for use later.

Building your cache will ultimately save you time, because you will always know where to look for the logo, your annual report stats, and statements to use in content creation that are filed by segmented audience or by service. To begin your cache, create the following folders:

- Logos in various formats and resolutions
- Logos from vendors to be used in materials (Overdrive, Freegal, OneClick, etc.).
- Copyright-free photos (organized by theme or library department) to be used in materials with a caption, source, and photographer's name.
- Head shots of key staff members with four-line bios, to be used with press releases or opinion pieces.
- Head shots of other key library stakeholders, such as your Friends or the Library president.
- Grant text—meaning any text that you might use repeatedly in grant writing. This includes the mission, vision statements, program descriptions, history of the organization, answers to frequently asked questions, etc.

- Any editorial or content master calendars, timelines, and core topics list.
- Your editorial language style guide (see below).
- Any standard layouts of templates for letters, PowerPoint slides, bookmarks, press releases, etc.
- Facts and stats sheet with current figures, such as your current material circulation number is 300,000; 1.2 million people walk through your doors every day; 25,000 eBooks were downloaded last year; etc.
- A login sheet with password links for all your social media channels. (You can lock this so that only certain people have the password to get in.)
- Photo model release forms—for adults and juvenile (see Appendix for sample); your library may want to have release form vetting through your legal folks
- Sample press release template (see Appendix for sample).
- A file where staff can store useful customer stories or anecdotes about the library.
- Annual reports.
- A file that contains your identity standards, usually put together by the graphic designer that designs your logo. These are the graphic design, social media channel, and website design standards that are used in your library system to form a cohesive visual identity, such as your name and logo, acceptable and unacceptable logo usage (never stretched, rotated, etc.), tagline, color palate (in CMYK, RGB, and HEX), fonts and typography, print collateral examples, ADA-compliant guidelines, and samples of your library cards, business cards, etc.
- Anything else that you constantly get asked to forward to someone.

As you start building your cache, be aware of standard good practices in marketing by avoiding marketing language that is clichéd, such as *new and improved*. Emphasize *benefits* rather than *features*. An easy way to distinguish whether it is a feature or a benefit is the *Batteries Included* example. Having batteries included in the new digital toy you buy is a feature or a factual statement about the program or service being promoted. A benefit statement would answer, "What's in it for me?" The benefit would be that I can start using my new toy right away and don't have to go to the store to buy batteries. To go even deeper into the benefit would be to think of it in terms of a result, or "I don't have to see the sad face on my child because I forgot to buy batteries." A library example of a feature versus benefit would be:

- **Feature:** Download eBooks from Your Library.
- **Benefit:** This means that you can save time, read it on multiple devices, change the font size to suit your eyes, and have it return automatically so you don't have overdue fees.

Think of statements that you might use to make your customers engaged or curious to learn more, or drop whatever they are doing and run to the library. If you are not sure what language to use, find a 12-year-old girl and ask her what she thinks about when you say, "Sign up today to use our new XYZ database!" Watch her eyes roll and confusion ensue.

To gain insights into what marketing language to add into your cache, tell her about a new service and have her explain it back to you and add in how she might use it. Audiotape or take notes on the language she uses, and parrot that language in your written documentation. Or use your own "So what?" testing, by adding *so what* to the end of any sentence you use. Test your language aloud in a conversation—people speak much differently from how they write, and you want any language that you use to come across as speakable.

Look through advertising from other libraries or nonprofits that you feel hit the mark. Some of my favorites include past *Library Journal* Library of the Year winners—Edmonton Public Library, Alberta, Canada; Salt Lake City Public Library, Utah; Columbus Metropolitan Library, Ohio; San Jose Public Library, California; and Queens Library, New York, among others. I also like to look up foreign libraries for a very different viewpoint—you don't have to be able to read it to see good design. For example, look at Stockholm Public Library, Sweden (https://biblioteket.stockholm.se). Some great nonprofit examples can be found through the Nonprofit Tech for Good website (http://nonprofittechforgood.com) that has numerous *best-of* examples.

Write down the headline and the positive benefit of the headline. Add that positive benefit into your marketing language cache. Ask questions of your customers and really listen to their responses, thinking about how the library can solve one of their problems. Conduct interviews and focus groups and videotape them so you can write those marketing language gems down later.

## Profile Your Audience

Your language cache should include some audience folders. Working through profiles of who you are talking to is the best way to decide what language to use when talking to them. If you have put together audience profiles from surveys, focus groups, demographic efforts, newsletter audience segmentations, or circulation statistics, you will want to reflect these groups and segments by naming your folders: " 'Tweens 8–12" or "Seniors 50+"; or, if you have done your homework and have segmented your customers by behaviors rather than demographics, you could title the folders *The Digitals* or *Caffeinates*.

Next, write down the key problems this audience faces. For example, do they need car repair, health information, or a quiet place to meet clients for their business? What benefits can the library offer to solve their problem? Write them down. Keep your files handy so you can add to them as you have those "a-ha" moments of insight during a meeting, or while riding the elevator. Use a list or note-taking app on your smartphone, so you can add ideas on the fly.

## Language Style

When composing marketing material, write in the first or second person as much as possible. When you refer to your library or system as *We* and your customers as *You*, you will automatically write in a more friendly, understandable tone. Learn to express opinions in your language; people look to libraries as being trustworthy leaders and experts in a variety of subjects. Remember that you want to make the library an approachable place. If you use an informal voice when writing, you many mistakenly leave out or misspell a word, say the wrong thing, or make some other mistake. Just excuse yourself in the comments box and go on—if you never make a mistake, you are probably spending way too much time on your updates, and people will think a robot is writing the posts. When the grammar-phobes correct you, just say "Thanks!"

Add in humor; or, if you don't feel you are funny, gather funny things related to your audience that are said by others and use them as quotes in your cache. Here are a few of my favorites:

- "People can lose their lives in libraries. They ought to be warned." —*Saul Bellow*
- "An original idea. That can't be too hard. The library must be full of them." —*Stephen Fry*
- "The truth is libraries are raucous clubhouses for free speech, controversy and community." —*Paula Poundstone*
- "Cutting libraries during a recession is like cutting hospitals during a plague." —*Eleanor Crumblehulme*
- "If truth is beauty, how come no one has their hair done in the library?" —*Lily Tomlin*
- "Being a writer in a library is rather like being a eunuch in a harem." —*John Braine*
- "A library is a place where you can lose your innocence without losing your virginity." —*Germaine Greer*
- "When the going gets tough, the tough get a librarian." —*Joan Bauer*

An organizational-language style guide should be a part of the overall style guide that comes from your branding guidelines. This style guide not only delineates how your organization will be referred to (such as whether you use an acronym, whether you have a short version of your name, or whether you always use the full name no matter what); or under what circumstances to use your tagline. There should also be written content on what type of voice, tone, and style you should use in your marketing content. Some types of language voice styles to consider are:

- Empathic
- Simplistic
- Journalistic
- Concise
- Authoritative
- Formal
- Casual

Having a concise personality or style documented can be helpful when you ask others to write content. It can also provide you with a starting point when you are under a time crunch to get something written.

Your language style guide should include anything that you find you edit over and over in someone else's writing.

- Do you use staff member's full names?
- Do you spell out numbers?
- Do you use AP or Chicago style for grammar questions?
- How do you format certain terms, such as e-book, Ebook, or eBook?
- Do you use periods in acronyms?
- Do you use "www" or "http://" with your web address?

Having a marketing language cache not only helps you and your staff, but also puts into writing some of your own style, which shows that your organization has a real live genuine person behind it. This is a very important part of your overall brand promise, and having it written down helps with consistency of marketing efforts, as well as with giving the next marketing director a guide after you leave to go on to bigger and better opportunities!

## TELLING YOUR STORY

One of the biggest shifts in the art and science of marketing strategies is the idea of telling your story through your marketing channels. This is one of the reasons that corporations and businesses align themselves with nonprofits. It gives them a more engaging way to tell their story than "We make the best widgets; you should buy them." With a library, you have the upper hand because libraries are all about stories—figuratively and literally!

In her book *The Fortune Cookie Principle* (2013), Bernadette Jiwa writes about why people will buy a fortune cookie even though they really don't taste any better than other cookies; it is because of—you guessed it—the fortune! "[T]he fortune is the magical, intangible part of the product or service, which is where the real value lies in the hearts and minds of the customer. The fortune is the story, the thing that makes people feel something." As marketers, we spend the majority of our time focusing on selling the cookie; what we really should be doing is creating better fortunes and telling our stories. So instead of always looking at the cookie, look inside and find the fortune that will make people care.

Giving people an emotional connection to the library helps define our common humanity, one that increases engagement, leading to increased support, advocacy, and contributions. When you hear a story, your brain goes to work automatically trying to relate the story to your own life experiences; this immediately builds a connection with you and the story. A great story doesn't tell what you do, but why you do it—the fortune. Ask yourself what the world would look like if libraries didn't exist, and answer that question with your story.

So what are your library's stories? How do you find them? Gather your library stories with the help of your staff. To help you sort through what would be a great story to share, look for stories that have these criteria:

- Shows what we have in common
- Focuses on one interesting person
- Shows a hardship that was overcome
- Makes others care about something

Use as many details as you can to make it real to your readers. Use specifics—hair color, clothes, and so on. Talk about the history or backstory of an individual. Show how their engagement with the library changed or transformed their life for the better. The ALA motto "Libraries Change Lives" is an effort to attract viewers to tell these library stories, and an even better motto might be "Libraries give people the knowledge to change their lives." One example of a great story was highlighted in an Information Today Special Report by Amber Clark (2009) on the "Across the Board" project conducted by the Leeds Library in the United Kingdom. "This project grew from the request of a local mother, Kate Webber, to get Boardmaker software in her library. The software is a series of picture-based programs that aids communication between parents and their autistic children. Since approximately 300 families in Leeds have children with autism (and an additional 25 preschool-age children there are diagnosed with the disorder every year), Webber's initial request eventually led to widespread use of the Boardmaker software throughout Leeds libraries. This set the stage for Across the Board to become an increasingly pertinent staple of the community" (Clark 2009). The story goes on to tell about who one mother of an autistic child helped to change the lives of many other families by partnering with her local library for this special software.

Also, there is this message shared by Amy Gilliland on the Libraries for Real Life website (http://www.librariesforreallife.org/stories/index.html):

> Without the library, I probably would have ended up a frustrated and unpleasant person. The library saved me and gave me worlds to explore beyond my own household. When I was 12, my parents separated and my mother and I moved to a small town in Colorado. It was 1974 and we knew no one. There was no radio, and the television only aired the Watergate hearings. My mother drank a lot and got involved with people that wanted nothing to do with me, and my schoolmates shunned an outsider. During my second week I found the library and spent three or more hours there every weekday. The librarians must have recognized how lost I was and found tasks for me to do so I felt useful. They saved up books for me to shelve. I ended up reading Vonnegut, philosophy, and feminist theory as well as many romance novels. I had somewhere to escape to instead of running away, drinking or taking drugs. We were only there six months but it set a pattern for my life. In any town I've ever lived in, I patronize the library and give back as a volunteer or a donor. Through the portal of my local branch, I've traveled all over the world and a few lively spots in the universe. My love of information has never ceased. This summer I will graduate with my doctorate degree, just shy of 50 years old—something I never could have done without the support of many helpful librarians. Thank you!" (Gilliland 2010)

These are published stories because a library had the advanced thought to get them down in writing. You have hundreds of these same stories in your library system, so figure out creative ways on how to bring them out and get them written down, and then use them to tell your library's story.

**MOXIE TIP** Make storytelling an agenda item for staff meetings. Everyone needs to add to the pool of stories. Assign different staff members to come up with stories for each meeting. Hearing these stories will not only develop a good understanding of storytelling, but will also give your staff a bond about the positive aspects of the mission of their jobs.

You can also gather stories through website surveys, writing contests, staff contests for story gathering, focus groups, or from anywhere you go to listen and talk to people. Ask them those questions that will bring out their own stories, then ask if you can share their story, either anonymously or with adding their name; the latter will make the story even stronger. Interview your staff for stories; ask them to tell you about the person they helped that they will never forget, or a memorable moment and what made it so memorable. Ask your board members why they choose to use their spare time volunteering for the library; or, if they had a million extra dollars in the budget, where they would spend it. Don't forget to ask people permission to publish their story; you can always change identifying details that are elements to the story if needed, or combine several stories into one.

## Storytelling Style

Something to consider while you are gathering your stories is the best way to tell a story. You can write about it on your blog, do an interview on your YouTube channel, feature it on your website, or write about it in your eNewsletter. So many channels to consider! Start by featuring the story on your blog, whether in text, photos, or video. When people go to a blog, they expect to read more than a 140-character post, and this larger framework provides a better space in which to tell your story. Use the story and its headline as a repurposed post on all of your other channels (e.g., Twitter, Facebook, etc.). This saves you time in content development and sends people to your blog as the hub of your marketing efforts. Make sure you provide a way for people to comment on the post without taking too much of their trouble. Those comments will help to drive up your search engine metrics.

Although it's best to have a consistent voice for promotional materials, with stories, you may want to change your style of writing or voice, depending on the type of story you have. Think about having an author persona for yourself as well as what persona you are writing for. Here are some persona archetype ideas to get you started:

- Expert: Are you or the person you are telling the story about an expert in something? What are the credibility factors you can bring in to gain trust and respect?
- Nerd: Similar to the expert, but it brings in a technology or geekiness factor.
- Jester: The comedian, who makes people laugh by sharing a funny view of the world.
- Explorer: Someone focused on being an individualist in the world, a goal orientation of climbing the highest peak, writing the greatest love story, etc.
- Child: A person who views the world through innocence and wonder.
- Sage: A persona that brings in the wisdom of the human condition.
- Commoner: An unassuming, friendly neighbor.

## Writing for an Emotional Pull

By using the fiction-writing techniques of a three-act structure, you will learn to write your story quickly and concisely.

- Act 1: Meet the main character and learn about their backstory and situation.
- Act 2: Define the situation further and show the obstacles and glimmer of hope that they find. What brings them into the library for help?
- Act 3: Focus on how they face the final obstacle and succeed at overcoming it (with the library's help).

Remember to keep the story about the characters, and not about the library. We are just in the supporting role (even if that role is Emmy-worthy). Powerful conflicts move the story ahead and add in the common humanity factor that drives emotions and moves your readers to an action.

Consider what emotions you want to evoke in your reader. Is it sadness, excitement, anger, happiness, or surprise? Also what action do you want them to take after reading the story? Should they check out more books on exercise? Should they go to your new car repair database? Or should they donate to a new fundraising effort? Not every story fits within the "crisis averted" scenario, but breaking it down into three acts that are all a paragraph long with a couple of quotes and pictures will give you the perfect blog post.

## WRITING MICRO-CONTENT

Practice writing headlines, subject lines, tweets, and other short snippets of content. This will not only help you save time, but it will also increase your "opens" and "shares." Use split testing, A-versus-B, headline segmentation in your email newsletter subject lines. Then track which subject line results in more people opening the email. Put together your top 10 list of subject lines, so you can refer to those and add them back into your content calendar to use later.

Are you stuck? Check out Getting Attention (http://www.gettingattention.org). In the past, this website has hosted a *best-of* tagline awards; some past winners are organizations like Librarians Without Borders, *Putting Information in the Hands of the World*; or Lake Champlain International (LCI), *Clean Water. Healthy Fish. Happy People.* See more at http://gettingattention.org/nonprofit-taglines/2012-nonprofit-tagline-award-winners.html. Look up the *Shorty Awards* (http://shortyawards.com), which shows the best producers of real-time short form content on social media across Twitter, Facebook, Tumblr, YouTube, Instagram, Vine, and more.

Staying away from spam trigger words is difficult. Most commercial email-sending services will have a spam checker so you can look to see what words in your content might be a trigger. Free is a great word for libraries to use. Just beware that using it in conjunction with other overused words, such as lose, freedom, stop, member, open, guarantee, and offer might trigger your email to go in the receiver's spam folder. But for social media short content, you should use positive response words in your headlines and subject lines such as Congratulations, New, Today, or Free. Look at the local news headlines and try to tie your Twitter headline to those to spark interest. Try to make the first six words in your subject line count; some longer lines may get cut off depending on the device that the person is viewing it on. Check to see if you only read the headline: do you understand what the post is about? Is the subject line or tweet benefit based for your customer, or is it all about you?

Give your reader a reason to want to read more. Make the headline or subject line about them and how will they benefit from reading your content; using the words *You* and *Your* will emphasize that. Asking a question is another good way to engage your reader. Make it short; this isn't essay writing. Edit a 16-word sentence down to seven words. Write something that piques interest—"The ten best loved stories of all time" or "How to save money on your car." Instead of "Join us tonight for the jazz concert at Public Branch, 7:00 p.m.," ramp up the moxie with "Shoo bob sho wadda yippity sha boom, Public Branch, today 7 pm, be there!"

There are millions of marketers sending out micro-content every day. Find the ones that resonate with you and see what words they use to grab or entice you. Make it a goal to spend more time on thinking out those subject headings on your eNewsletters rather than just filling it in the second before you send it.

## WHEN TO SAY GOODBYE

After years of trying to get someone to like your Facebook page, after reading hundreds of online documents giving you the 10 ways to gain 10,000 friends in a month, and doing the step-by-step guidelines to no avail or after finding that everyone has switched over to the newest, shiniest social media app, how do you know it is time to pull the plug on your channel?

If you have decided that one of your social network accounts is not worth maintaining because it has been up for at least a year, it has been promoted through all of your other channels, and your metric analyses still have not changed or are losing ground, maybe this channel is just not going to work for you and your customers. There are good and bad ways of dropping the account. The worst way you can do it is just to never post anything again, leaving it stagnant, and leaving people wondering what happened. The best way is to post a final message that explains that there won't be any further updates, or that you are moving to a new network, and point them to the new channel. You should also turn off the comments section and the ability for others to post so you do not have lingering comments or spamming out on the Internet that will show up on searches. You should not drop or close the account totally. Who's to say the social media swings in popularity might not come back around to that channel, or that they might do a major developmental change that will ramp it up again. In any case, you wouldn't want to lose the channel name so that someone else claiming your handle could start back up and impersonate you.

Marketing can and should be a lot of work up front. Whether it's a marketing plan, branding, getting buy-in, or interacting with the community, all this work up front will mean a more streamline implementation later. Included in this work is the marketing language cache—stories, quotes, taglines, logo, statements, anything that you may need to refer to or use in your marketing process. Add folders that have specific language and images for age groups and types of customers. This will make an even easier referral system. Use language like "we," "our," and "yours" to create a more friendly tone. Having a consistent style will not only save you time, but also give staff a clearer picture of what language to use. Stories can invoke strong emotions in those reading them. Use stories to create buy-in from your staff and board members. As you gather stories and review, think about what method of sharing them might be the most consistent with the stories' content. Stories make it okay to have a changing voice. They may help to add dimension to your marketing by giving the customer another voice to resonate with. This resonance can also be helped by invoking emotions. This chapter lays out an easy three-act storyline that will enhance the pull. Keep in mind what emotions you are trying to raise as you create your acts. Subject lines, headlines, and tweets are all part of micro-content. Add this type of brainstorming to your cache to not only help you save time in the future, but enhance your skill in creating this type of content. And, as always, mold that one-on-one relationship by making your lines and titles all about *them*!

## REFERENCES

Clark, A. (2009). "Special Report: Libraries Change Lives Award Goes to Leeds Project That Serves Autistic Children." Information Today, Inc., September–October. http://www.infotoday.com/mls/sep09/Clark.shtml.

Gilliland, A. (2010). Comment in "Stories to Read." Libraries for Real Life. http://www.librariesforreallife.org/stories/index.html.

Jiwa, B. (2013). *The Fortune Cookie Principle*. Australia: The Story of Telling Press.

# FINAL THOUGHTS

As a full-time library marketer, I began this book with the idea of sharing some of what I have learned over the years with others who might find themselves having to market their libraries due to decreases in funding, increases in competition, or just because they want to make sure that libraries stay relevant into the next century. After reading this book, I hope you have picked out some marketing strategies that jumped out at you right away and made you think, "I could use that idea for our new ABC service." Make a commitment to doing something new this week to get yourself out of your marketing rut. Make sure your library is set up for success by starting with a comprehensive marketing plan and content calendar—even if you only have time to do it for one program or service, get it done so that you can start testing your assumptions, gathering data, and seeing what the next steps need to be.

Beware of all the shiny new tools. As fun and engaging as social media is, if it is not your cup of tea, find someone else to help you who has a passion for it. Doing something that ramps up your moxie and makes you feel on top of the marketing world will always turn out better than something that you feel you have to do because everyone else is doing it. Make your customers expect and demand that same level of amazing customer service at your library as they would find at a competing bookstore. The basics of not only good, but amazing customer service by the library staff will do more for your marketing plan than 1,000 Facebook posts.

Our goal as library marketers is not only to convey to people the rich resources we have to offer them, but how it will make their lives better. If we were able to ensure that everyone who currently has a library card continues to use it, and that our potential users sign up for one and use it, we will never have to worry about the future of the library. Ned Potter (2012) states that "Being a librarian has always been about finding the right information, for the right people, at the right time. Marketing a library is really just about promoting the right benefits of that information, to the right people, at the right time." You are probably on the right track, and that is why you have invested your time in reading books like this one. Set yourself a weekly goal to keep the momentum going. For example, you might go through and sign up for all the social media channels you think you might be using in the future to hold your vanity URL before someone else reserves it. You could create more than one content example to go with various audience segments, or try measuring a new metric for a channel that you have never fully dissected. Go through your library, take down all the signage, and decide how to either make them more customer-friendly, or decide if they are needed at all. "Good marketing results in libraries being used more, libraries being used better, libraries being valued more highly, and libraries proving to the people who matter that they should not become a target for cuts. The only way to predict the future of libraries is to dictate it ourselves" (Potter 2012).

The goal of moxie marketing should be to create a demand of high expectations and evangelistic loyalty by your countless customers, patrons, members, and friends. This is true whether you are located in the high plains of Colorado with limited Internet access or in a metropolis with high-speed broadband, if your marketing plan includes outreach to the homeless or outreach to million-dollar donors. Don't forget, moxie marketing is fun! If you look at all of this just as work, you are doing it wrong. If you feel like you are becoming addicted, that is a good sign! If you find yourself getting bogged down in your never-ending to-do lists, here are a couple of fun and quick ideas to energize you and ramp it up.

1. Switch up your 404 webpage. Do you have a boring 404 error message as your standard response to a page not found or a broken link—something like "404 Not Found"? Ramp it up by adding some personality to your message. Have your IT person help you by branding the page image with your library's identity as well as changing the message to "You found it! Our 404 page, we have been looking all over for it, thank you so much!" and adding in a photo of your executive director or library mascot. Somewhere along the way, people have decided that the library is a stuffy institution, which follows with the never-ending idea of the eyeglass- and bun-wearing shushing librarian. Some of my favorite posts of late that show some true moxie are the ones that include the tattooed librarians as well as the "Shh! Happens at Your Library" slogan making the rounds, trying to address these stereotypes.

2. Add some delight to your audience's day by being unexpected. Send out an email in the words of Jane Austen talking about her latest adventure of riding her horse through the snow. Or a personal heartfelt message from your book on hold about how it can't wait to meet you, and hopes to see you soon.

3. Show a side of the library that is unexpected and shows there are real people working there. Don't take yourself too seriously; show the library in a fun, interesting light by adding a board to your Pinterest site highlighting funny questions asked or comments overheard in the library. Name your board "They Said What?!!" Find humorous photos to go along with the questions such as "Why were so many Civil War battles fought on National Park sites?" or found inside a DVD case the note "To save you from the same disappointment I had, this movie does not have a happy ending." There is even a blog called *I Work at a Public Library* by Gina Sheridan (http://www.iworkatapubliclibrary.com) if you need some ideas to get you started, but I am sure that you hear about these comments every day.

4. Don't forget, it is all about them. Send out a "Happy Anniversary!" card (snail or email) to someone who has had their library card for a year. Celebrate your customers by making their day brighter and in turn making yours.

Remember that social media is about being social. It is about building relationships with individuals instead of reaching the masses by the "spray and pray" advertising of the past. When you are uploading your library video to YouTube, or posting your status update to Facebook, it all comes down not to how many followers you have, but to how you connect with those followers. Creating those personal interactions not only will help people learn about the library, but will also help the library learn about their customers. Social media helps in spreading your message to people outside your normal customer base at a faster pace than a great book display or poster hanging in the foyer. Don't forget to show your personality and humanness (both positive and negative).

How do you know if you are doing it right? The fun of working in this crazy, diverse field sometimes makes you wonder if, at the end of the day, you are doing your job right. You can measure the effectiveness of campaigns and tactics, you can count the attendance at programs, you can look at your metrics of likes and shares, but how do you know if the time you put in is making a difference? In the *Nonprofit Marketing Guide* (2010), Kivi Leroux Miller suggests that you ask yourself these questions:

- Does everything you are doing help to make your library stand out from the crowd?
- Is your library perceived as a leader or expert?
- Do your current supporters and customers remember who you are?
- Do your customers think of you favorably?
- Are you connecting with new people?
- And, perhaps the most important, do you love your job?

If you can answer yes to all of these questions, then you can give yourself a pat on the back and say "Great job! You are a moxie marketer!"

I love this crazy marketing business, I love the idea generation and brainstorming, I love the content curation and creative process of repurposing content for different channels. I love getting entrenched in new social media networks and gathering the metrics and data behind them to see how they are working. I love reading about new technologies and what the coming trends are. So I guess it all boils down to I love my job, and I hope this book helps to spread that enthusiasm out to you!

## REFERENCES

Leroux Miller, K. (2010). *The Nonprofit Marketing Guide: High-Impact, Low-Cost Ways to Build Support for Your Good Cause*. San Francisco: Jossey-Bass.

Potter, N. (2012). *The Library Marketing Toolkit*. London: Facet Publishing.

# APPENDIX

## CHAPTER 1

**Your Public Library—Sample Marketing Plan A**

**Library Mission Statement:**

A) State the purpose of the marketing plan
B) Explain the "why" (Golden Circle Concept by Simon Sinek)

  1. Why does the Library exist?

  2. How do you accomplish the "why"

  3. What is it that you do (to accomplish how and why)?

**Description of your current program or service:**

**SWOT Analysis:**

  *Strengths*

  *Weaknesses*

  *Opportunities*

  *Threats*

**Marketing Goals**

  Based upon the SWOT analysis, create 3 or 4 goals for the year.
  For example:

  Goal 1: To increase children's attendance at storytime by 25%

  Goal 2:

  Goal 3:

**Who are you marketing to?** (Your audience segment):

  Goal 1: Parents and caregivers of children under 5 years of age.

  Goal 2:

  Goal 3:

**What strategy will you use to accomplish this goal?**

  Goal 1: Partner with local childcare facilities to do outreach storytimes once a month.

  Benefit: Working parents who cannot bring their children to the library.

  Goal 2:

  Goal 3:

**Budget**

  Goal 1: We will redo existing storytimes so that the only cost associated would be two hours
    of staff time: approx. $50.
  Goal 2:
  Goal 3:

**Your Public Library—Sample Marketing Plan B**

| Goal | To increase children's attendance at Storytimes by 25% | | | | | | |
|---|---|---|---|---|---|---|---|
| | Target Segment: Parents and caregivers of children under 5 years of age. | | | | | | |

| Strategies and Tactics | Timeline | Who? | Media Channels | Measurement | Status updates | Budget | Outcomes |
|---|---|---|---|---|---|---|---|
| Partner with local childcare facilities to do outreach storytimes once a month<br>• Flyers out to parents announcing storytimes<br>• Newsletters<br>• Blog post | Pilot program between August 2014 to May 2015 | – Lead: Marketing Manager<br>– Second: Outreach Manager | Newsletter Blog Post Flyer Website | Count storytime attendance | WK1<br>• Team established<br>WK2<br>• Team meetings<br>• Programming near finalized<br>• Web page updated<br>WK3<br>• Designed and distributed promotional flyers | $50 to come from Marketing Budget | Desired outcome:<br>• Increase children's attendance at storytimes<br>• Showcase programs and services inside and outside the library |

## CHAPTER 3

Sample Program Feedback Form

# What do you think?

**Program:** _____ **Date:** _____

POUDRE RIVER
PUBLIC LIBRARY
DISTRICT

*Please circle program location:*
Old Town    Harmony    Council Tree

Outside the Library

◆ How would you rate this program?
  □ Excellent    □ Very Good    □ Good    □ Fair    □ Poor

◆ How would you rate the presenter(s)?
  □ Excellent    □ Very Good    □ Good    □ Fair    □ Poor

◆ How would you rate the presenter's knowledge of the subject?
  □ Excellent    □ Very Good    □ Good    □ Fair    □ Poor

◆ What would you change? _____

◆ Did this program give you useful new information?
  □ Yes    □ Maybe    □ No
  How will you use this information? _____

◆ Did this program help to improve an aspect of your life?
  □ Yes    □ Maybe    □ No
  *more space for comments on back*

**Sign me up for the weekly email of events & monthly newsletter!**
  □ Adult    □ Teen    □ Child

◆ Name: _____
◆ Email: _____

*How did you learn
about this program?*
□ Newspaper
    Which one? _____
□ Monthly Newsletter
□ Word of mouth
□ Web Calendar
□ Library Email
□ Facebook
□ Twitter
□ Website
    Which one? _____
Other (specify) _____

## CHAPTER 9

### Sample Photo Release Form

**Our Wonderful Library Logo Here**

**Photo Release:**

Please sign two copies of this agreement, return one copy to the library, and retain one for your files.

As the parent/legal guardian (circle one) of the minor student, _____,

I hereby give my consent to the Library Name to photograph this minor student and to use such photograph to promote Library programs and events. This may include but is not limited to printing the photograph of this minor student to accompany a printed article or other material from the Library, describing the pictured event in which he or she participated. This includes allowing the photograph to appear on the library web page via the Internet or in Library sponsored social media posts. I understand that such photographs remain the property of the Library Name.

        Activity or Event_____

           Yes, I do give permission. No, I do not give permission.

_____

First and last name of parent/guardian (Please print legibly)

_____

Street Address        City        State        Zip

_____

Signature        Date

**Sample Press Release**

_____ **PRESS RELEASE**

**FOR IMMEDIATE RELEASE**
**September 24, 2016**        CONTACT:You

                        Communications Manager
                        Phone
                        Email

### WRITERS' BLOCK

**YOUR TOWN, State.** – On Saturday, **September 26**, from **Noon to 3 pm**, the BEST LIBRARY IN THE WORLD will be sponsoring "Writers' Block" at XYZ Library, ADDRESS.

    Write history! Come, grab a piece of chalk, and contribute to Fort Collins' first community created story. Join with local authors, family, neighbors and friends for a day of scribbling a creative story on the sidewalk around XYZ Library. Let out your inner author, and enjoy an afternoon of fun and writing. Everyone is a writer at Writers' Block!

Be a part of history and make your mark at "Writers' Block." There will be music by the Z Mountain Rangers bluegrass band and authors to visit, while you wait to make your mark on the pavement at this fun community event. The story will be digitally filmed and shared through various means following the event.

Be There. Be Square.

This program is free and open to the public, everyone is welcome to participate. For more information, please visit BEST LIBRARY IN THE WORLD WEB SITE OR CALL 234-456-7891

###

# GLOSSARY

**Analytics:** The statistics generated to track which website pages are viewed, what links are clicked on, and how they found the site. Analytics are also used in email.

**Annotations:** These are messages overlaid on YouTube videos that are clickable and can link to other websites.

**Audience Retention:** The metric that tells you the average time duration of a viewer watching a YouTube video.

**Blog:** An online journal that is updated with the most recent entries at the top. Comes from the term "web log."

**Bounce:** In the case of email, this is when the email is sent but not received and is returned to the sender. Bounce rate, as it applies to a webpage, is if someone hits the page and then goes somewhere else.

**Circles:** These are the clusters of a user's friends on Google+.

**Conversation/mention:** This refers to reach in the sense of how often the library is talked about; normally, the higher the number, the better.

**Engagement:** From a metrics perspective, this is the number of people who have interacted with the social media channel by commenting, liking, sharing, etc.

**Handle:** This is the username you use on Twitter.

**Impressions:** A marketing term used in both mass media and social media marketing referring to the number of people who have had a certain piece of content show up in their news feed.

**Infographic:** A visual that represents information or data usually used to simplify complex pieces of information.

**Insights:** The page on Facebook that shows all of your analytic information.

**Lurker:** A person who reads discussions and other interactive social media but rarely or never participates in the discussion.

**Meme:** An image, video, or piece of text that is copied and spread by Internet users, usually referring to the images that you see in social media that have text "comments" overlaid on the top of them.

**Open Rate:** The percentage of email recipients who opened the email message.

**+1:** This is the Google+ way of saying they appreciate the content you posted.

**Profile:** The page created to represent the individual or organization.

**Reach:** The number of people who saw a piece of content on their Facebook or LinkedIn newsfeed (this doesn't mean the person has interacted with the content). Facebook has restricted the organic reach to users, although user sharing of content can increase reach.

**Referrals:** Refers to how many visitors to your website are coming from a social media site. Part of the analytics number.

**Response Rate:** As it pertains to social media, this is calculated by examining the number of questions or comments being posted on a Facebook wall, then seeing how many replies to those questions are received. Also calculated by the number of mentions on Twitter.

**Retweet:** The act of forwarding some else's Twitter "tweet" to your own followers.

**RSS Feed:** Real Simple Syndication (RSS) is a way that a website can send new content automatically to a subscriber through an RSS application reader.

**SEO:** Search Engine Optimization, which is the process of improving the volume of people coming to your webpage from the various search engines.

**Sharing:** This refers to how many times your content is shared by others, such retweeting on Twitter.

**Tags:** Categorizing an article or blog entry with a descriptive keyword so that it can be easily searched for in search engines.

**URL:** Unified Resource Language, a long name for what is really just a web "address."

# SUGGESTED READING
# AND RESOURCES

## BOOKS

Berger, J. (2013). *Contagious: Why Things Catch On*. New York: Simon & Schuster.

Crawford, W. (2014). *Successful Social Networking in Public Libraries*. Chicago: ALA Editions.

Giuseppe, I. (2006). *The Power of Survey Design: A User's Guide for Managing Surveys, Interpreting Results, and Influencing Respondents*. Washington, DC: World Bank Publications.

Godin, S. (1999). *Permission Marketing: Turning Strangers into Friends and Friends into Customers*. New York: Simon & Schuster.

Godin, S. (2007). *Purple Cow: Transform Your Business by Being Remarkable*. New York: Penguin Books.

Gubniskais, V., Harrod, K. & Smallwood, C. (Eds.). (2012). *Marketing Your Library: Tips and Tools That Work*. Jefferson, NC: McFarland & Company.

Gunelius, S. (2011). *30-Minute Social Media Marketing*. New York: McGraw-Hill.

Hughes, M. (2005). *Buzzmarketing: Get People to Talk about Your Stuff*. New York: Penguin Group.

Jiwa, B. (2013). *The Fortune Cookie Principle*. CreateSpace Independent Publishing Platform.

Johnson, S. (2010). *Where Good Ideas Come From: The Natural History of Innovation*. New York: Riverhead Books.

Kabani, S. (2010). *The Zen of Social Media Marketing: The Easier Way to Build Credibility, Generate Buzz, and Increase Revenue*. Dallas, TX: Benbella Books.

Leroux Miller, K. (2010). *The Nonprofit Marketing Guide*. San Francisco: Jossey-Bass.

Leroux Miller, K. (2013). *Content Marketing for Nonprofits*. San Francisco: Jossey-Bass.

Levinson, J. C. (2010). *Guerrilla Marketing for Nonprofits: 250 Tactics to Promote, Motivate, and Raise More Money*. Irvine, CA: Entrepreneur Press.

Mansfield, H. (2012). *Social Media for Social Good: A How-to Guide for Nonprofits*. New York: McGraw-Hill.

Mathos, M., & Norman, C. (2012). *Social Media Tactics for Nonprofits: A Field Guide*. Hoboken, NJ: John Wiley & Sons.

Newman, D. (2013). *Do It! Marketing*. New York: American Management Association.

Potter, N. (2012). *The Library Marketing Toolkit*. London: Facet Publishing.

Rosen, N. (2012). *Chatter Marketing*. Austin, TX: Emerald Book Company.

Sernovitz, A. (2006). *Word-of-Mouth Marketing: How Smart Companies Get People Talking.* Chicago: Kaplan Publishing.

Siess, J. (2003). *The Visible Librarian: Asserting Your Value with Marketing and Advocacy.* Chicago: American Library Association.

Solomon, L. (2013). *The Librarian's Nitty-Gritty Guide to Social Media.* Chicago: ALA Editions.

Stephenson, J., & Thurman, C. (2007). *Ultimate Small Business Marketing Guide.* Irvine, CA: Entrepreneur Press.

Stratten, S. (2014). *QR Codes Kill Kittens: How to Alienate Customers, Dishearten Employees and Drive Your Business into the Ground.* Hoboken, NJ: John Wiley & Sons.

Thompson, L. (2013). *Creative Conspiracy: The New Rules of Breakthrough Collaboration.* Boston: Harvard Business Review Press.

Thomsett-Scott, B. (Ed.). (2014). *Marketing with Social Media.* Chicago: Library and Information Technology Association, ALA TechSource.

Vaynerchuk, G. (2013). *Jab, Jab, Jab, Right Hook: How to Tell Your Story in a Noisy Social World.* New York: HarperBusiness.

## WEB READING

Breed, Elizabeth. (2013, March–April). "Creating a Social Media Policy: What We Did, What We Learned." *Information Today* 27(2). http://www.infotoday.com/mls/mar13/Breed—Creating-a-social-media-policy.shtml. An article showing the evolution of a social media policy and guidelines at the Capital Area District Library in Michigan.

Dempsey, Kathy. *Libraries Are Essential.* http://www.librariesareessential.com. The website has a great list of library marketing resources as well as the Marketing Library Services newsletter (subscription cost); see also the M Word Blog at http://www.themwordblog.blogspot.com.

"Descriptive Adjectives Vocabulary List." http://www.myvocabulary.com/word-list/descriptive-adjectives-vocabulary. A list of descriptive adjectives to use in your writing, when you need a boost.

Johnson, Steven. (2010). "Where Good Ideas Come From." YouTube video, 4:06, posted by RiverheadBooks. https://www.youtube.com/watch?v=NugRZGDbPFU.

Kilroy, Dana. (2014, July 29). "Is Your Facebook Contest Legal?" Socially Stacked. http://www.sociallystacked.com/2014/07/is-your-facebook-contest-legal-infographic. Infographic explaining contest entry dos and don'ts on Facebook, as of July 2014.

LinkedIn for Good (official blog). http://blog.linkedin.com/topic/linkedin-for-good. Offers articles featuring great ways in which nonprofits are using this application.

Miller, Kivi Leroux. Nonprofit Marketing Gude.com. http://www.nonprofitmarketingguide.com.

Nonprofit Tech for Good. http://nonprofittechforgood.com.

Open Education Database. "Your Brain on Books: 10 Things That Happen to Our Minds When We Read." http://oedb.org/ilibrarian/your-brain-on-books-10-things-that-happen-to-our-minds-when-we-read. A collection of online college ranking that also has some good library-focused information through their iLibrarian Blog site.

TechSoup, http://www.Techsoup.org: Forum, blog, and topics of interest for libraries.

Walter, Ekaterina. "The Best and Worst of Real-Time Marketing: 4 Lessons for Marketers." http://m.fastcompany.com/3031542/hit-the-ground-running/the-best-and-worst-of-real-time-marketing-4-lessons-for-marketers.

Word of Mouth Marketing Association. http://www.womma.org. Sign up for their great eNewsletter.

### Social Media Industry Blogs Packed with Tips and Tricks

- PR Daily. http://www.prdaily.com.
- Social Media Examiner. http://www.socialmediaexaminer.com.

## RESOURCES

### Audio

- Audacity (http://audacity.sourceforge.net): Open-source, cross-platform free tool for audio recording and editing.
- Auphonic (https://auphonic.com): Tool for web-based podcasts, radio shows, etc. Free for two hours of audio processed per month, but more can be purchased.
- BlogTalkRadio (http://www.blogtalkradio.com): Simple online platform for recording and hosting podcasts.
- NewBlue Audio Scrubber (http://www.newbluefx.com/product/scrubbers): Software-based audio scrubber to help with repairing sound quality.

### DIY Graphic Design Tools

- Canva (https://www.canva.com): Create graphics, quote pictures, and infographics.
- Over (https://itunes.apple.com/us/app/over/id535811906?mt=8): Mobile app to create text overlays on photos.
- Photobucket (http://photobucket.com): Upload photos and edit with filters and effects.
- PicMark (http://www.picmark.co): Add a watermark to your photo or image before sharing it online.
- PicMonkey (http://picmonkey.com): For text and image graphics, it includes templates for common social media banners and headers.
- QuotesCover.com (http://www.quotescover.com): Used to make text and image memes.
- TinEye (https://www.tineye.com): A reverse image search tool. Upload an image and it can find the original source; very helpful for copyright compliance

### Creating Infographics

- Easy WebContent Presenter (http://easywebcontent.com/blog/easy-webcontent-presenter-is-open-beta-create-free-html5-presentations-and-animations)
- Infogr.am (http://infogr.am)
- Piktochart (http://piktochart.com): Offers a variety of templates. Free and paid versions.
- Timeline (http://readwritethink.org/files/resources/interactives/timeline_2): Create graphical, interactive timelines of items or events.
- Tiki-Toki (http://www.tiki-toki.com): Multimedia interactive timelines; basic version is free.
- Venngage (https://venngage.com)
- Visual.ly (http://visual.ly): A marketplace for finding great design ideas and tips.

### Editorial Calendar Templates

- Content Marketing Institute, Editorial Calendar (http://contentmarketinginstitute.com/2010/08/content-marketing-editorial-calendar): Template link in center of the page.
- Edit Flow (http://editflow.org): A free WordPress plugin with editorial calendar and workflow management.

- HubSpot (http://offers.hubspot.com/blog-editorial-calendar): In exchange for joining an email list, you can download an Excel file calendar template as well as other templates.

## Fonts

- Font Squirrel (http://fontsquirrel.com): Free downloadable fonts for commercial use.
- UrbanFonts (http://www.urbanfonts.com): Includes many free fonts.

## Photos

Most are cost and royalty free with proper attribution.

- Creative Commons (http://www.creativecommons.org)
- ImageAfter.com
- iStock (gives away free photos every week)
- Photopin
- PublicDomainPictures.net

## Surveys and Polls

- Poll Everywhere (http://www.polleverywhere.com): Great for live presentations, real-time interactive polling or quizzes; the audience answers by text message. Free version up to 40 responses per poll, templates, live word clouds and more.
- Quibblo (http://www.quibblo.com): Great for making short engaging quizzes or polls to share on social media.
- SlimSurveys (https://slimsurveys.com): Templates for short online surveys, mobile-ready for customer feedback on single topics.
- SurveyMonkey (http://surveymonkey.com): Free version allows up to 10 questions and 100 responses. Paid accounts add many more features including custom identity branding and A/B testing.
- Zoho Surveys (http://www.zoho.com/survey): Just one of the business applications by Zoho. Free and paid versions.

## Video

- Animoto (http://animoto.com): This takes still shots and combines them into a video with music and special effects. Free and paid versions.
- Camtasia (http://www.techsmith.com/camtasia.html): Software that helps with screen captures or screencast videos, mobile video capture; especially good for longer training videos.
- Jing (http://www.techsmith.com/jing.html): Free downloadable software that does short screen captures and screencast videos.

## Video Editing

- FlixMaster (http://www.flixmaster.com): Cloud-based editing and publishing.
- Magisto (http://magisto.com): Turns photos and videos into movies with built-in themes.
- Windows Live Movie Maker: Comes preinstalled on many Windows PCs.
- YouTube Editor (http://youtube.com/editor): Conduct basic editing, adjust audio levels, and add effects and soundtracks within YouTube.

## Webinar Tools and Live Screen Sharing and Recording

- Adobe Connect
- AnyMeeting.com
- FreeConferenceCall.com
- FreeScreenSharing
- GoToWebinar
- JoinMe
- WebEx

## Word Clouds

- Tagul (https://tagul.com): Fancier word clouds in shapes, fonts and colors. Can be saved in PNG format.
- Wordle (http://www.wordle.net/create): Generates a word cloud from any text you input.

## Writing

- StoryBoard That (http://storyboardthat.com): An online storyboard creation tool using drag-and-drop interface and graphic organizer for telling a linear story.
- Storybook (http://storybook.en.softonic.com): Helps you to organize threads of storylines, characters, etc. Color-coded graphic organizer (not a word processor), open-source application.

*Many thanks to Jennifer E. Burke at IntelliCraft Research for many of these suggestions.*

# INDEX

## About the Author

PAULA WATSON-LAKAMP is Communications Manager for Poudre River Public Library District, Fort Collins, Colorado. She has a background in communications, marketing, special events, graphic design, brand management, and social media. Paula owned her own marketing and design business and has worked for nonprofits and city governments over the past three decades. Paula has a passion for "pushing the envelope" and sees marketing and promotions as fun, creative endeavors that can be enjoyed by all.